# Jokes Women
# **Won't**
# Laugh At

*Berkley Books by Tom Hobbes*

JOKES MEN WON'T LAUGH AT
JOKES WOMEN WON'T LAUGH AT

# Jokes Women **Won't** Laugh At

# Tom Hobbes

BERKLEY BOOKS, NEW YORK

Many thanks to all who contributed jokes, including Andy, Bill, Doc, Doug, Ho, Howard, Jeremy, Jimmy, Ken, Michael, Phil, Paul, Ratso, Roz, and everyone at Gates Restaurant.

**THE BERKLEY PUBLISHING GROUP**
**Published by the Penguin Group**
**Penguin Group (USA) Inc.**
**375 Hudson Street, New York, New York 10014, USA**
Penguin Group (Canada), 90 Eglinton Avenue East, Suite 700, Toronto, Ontario M4P 2Y3, Canada
(a division of Pearson Penguin Canada Inc.)
Penguin Books Ltd., 80 Strand, London WC2R 0RL, England
Penguin Group Ireland, 25 St. Stephen's Green, Dublin 2, Ireland (a division of Penguin Books Ltd.)
Penguin Group (Australia), 250 Camberwell Road, Camberwell, Victoria 3124, Australia
(a division of Pearson Australia Group Pty. Ltd.)
Penguin Books India Pvt. Ltd., 11 Community Centre, Panchsheel Park, New Delhi—110 017, India
Penguin Group (NZ), 67 Apollo Drive, Rosedale, North Shore 0632, New Zealand
(a division of Pearson New Zealand Ltd.)
Penguin Books (South Africa) (Pty.) Ltd., 24 Sturdee Avenue, Rosebank, Johannesburg 2196,
South Africa

Penguin Books Ltd., Registered Offices: 80 Strand, London WC2R 0RL, England

JOKES WOMEN WON'T LAUGH AT

A Berkley Book / published by arrangement with the author

PRINTING HISTORY
Berkley edition / June 2002

Copyright © 2002 by Tom Hobbes.
Cover design by Pyrographx.
Interior text design by Kristin del Rosario.

ISBN: 978-0-425-18519-3

BERKLEY®
Berkley Books are published by The Berkley Publishing Group,
a division of Penguin Group (USA) Inc.,
375 Hudson Street, New York, New York 10014.
BERKLEY® is a registered trademark of Penguin Group (USA) Inc.
The "B" design is a trademark of Penguin Group (USA) Inc.

PRINTED IN THE UNITED STATES OF AMERICA

20   19   18   17   16   15   14   13   12   11   10

Ah, women. The fairer sex. The better half. They're wives, they're girlfriends, they're mistresses, coworkers, and even bosses. You can't live with them, and you can't live without them. When they're happy, you're happy. In part, it's because when they're *un*happy they can make your life a living hell. When they're *un*happy, they can make *your* life not worth living at all. And one other thing. Let's face it, they control the commodity. That's *the* commodity—the only one you really care about. Sex.

When you're not enjoying the company of women, or how they look, or how they act, or how much fun you can have with them, you may also enjoy laughing about them. That's the reason we wrote this book—for your enjoyment. But just don't show it to any of the women in your life, because there's one thing we can promise you. These are *jokes women won't laugh at.* And if you share them with the women you know, they may never speak to you again.

—Tom Hobbes

**Q:** WHY DO WOMEN RUB THEIR EYES WHEN THEY WAKE UP?

**A:** Because they don't have balls to scratch.

A man is in a hotel lobby. He wants to ask the clerk a question. As he turns to go to the front desk, he accidentally bumps into a woman beside him, and as he does, his elbow hits her in the breast, startling both of them.

The man turns to her and says, "Ma'am, if your heart is as soft as your breast, I know you'll forgive me."

She replies, "If your penis is as hard as your elbow, I'm in Room 1128."

**Q:** WHAT'S A LESBIAN DINOSAUR?
**A:** A Lickalotapus.

**Q:** WHAT'S A RODEO FUCK?
**A:** When you've got your wife down on all fours, and you're about to enter her doggy style, and you say, "This is the way your sister likes it, too!"

1

A guy goes to pick up his date for the evening. She's not ready yet, so he has to sit in the living room with her parents. He has a bad case of gas and really needs to relieve some pressure. Then the family dog jumps up on the couch next to him. He decides that he can let a little fart out, and if anyone notices, they will think that the dog did it. He farts, and the woman yells, "Spot, get down from there."

The guy thinks, "Great, they think the dog did it." He releases another fart, and the woman again yells for the dog to get down. This goes on for a couple more farts. Finally, the woman yells, "Damn it, Spot, get down before he shits on you."

**Q:** WHY CAN'T YOU TELL WOMEN KNOCK-KNOCK JOKES?
**A:** Because they always leave to answer the door.

A man went to see his doctor, who asked him for a urine sample, a stool sample, and a semen sample. The man said, "Doc, I'm in kind of a hurry today. Can I just leave my underwear with you?"

A couple were celebrating their fiftieth wedding anniversary, so they decided to return to the little town where they first met. They sat in a small coffee shop in the town and were telling the waitress about their love for each other and how they met at this same spot. Sitting next to them was the local cop, and he smiled as the old couple spoke.

After the waitress left the table, the old man said to his wife, "Remember the first time we made love? It was up in that field across the road, when I had you against the fence. Why don't we do it again for old times' sake?"

The wife giggled and said, "Sure, why not?"

So they went out the door and across to the field. The cop smiled to himself, thinking how romantic this was, and decided he'd better keep an eye on the couple so they didn't run into any harm.

The old couple walked to the field, and as they approached the fence they began to undress. The old man picked up his wife when they were naked and leaned her against the fence.

The cop was watching from the bushes and was surprised at what he saw. The wife bounced up and down excitedly while the husband thrashed around like a wild man. At the end, they both fell to the ground in exhaustion.

Eventually, they stood up, shook themselves, and got dressed. As they walked back toward the road, the cop stepped from his hiding spot and said, "That was the most wonderful lovemaking I have ever seen. You must have been a wild couple when you were young."

"Not really," said the old man. "When we were young, that fence wasn't electrified."

A woman, wanting to earn some money, decided to hire herself out as a handyman-type and started canvassing a wealthy neighborhood. She went to the front door of the first house and asked the owner if he had any jobs for her to do. "Well, you can paint my porch. How much will you charge?"

The woman said, "How about fifty dollars?" The man agreed and told her that the paint and ladders that she might need were in the garage. A short time later, the woman came to the door to collect her money.

"You're finished already?" he asked.

"Yes," she answered, "and I had paint left over, so I gave it two coats." Impressed, the man reached in his pocket for the fifty dollars.

"And by the way," she added, "that's not a Porch, it's a Mercedes."

Two guys walking down the street spot a dog licking his privates.

"I wish I could do that," one says.

"Don't," the other replies. "The dog would bite you."

Down on their luck, a couple decides the only way to pay the rent is for the woman to turn to prostitution. Her husband drives her to a street corner and explains the pricing schedule: "A hand job is forty dollars, and a blow job is a hundred."

"Okay," the wife says. She walks around the corner, and there she finds a young man, whom she propositions. After seeing what he has under his pants, she runs back around the corner to her husband.

"Can I borrow a hundred bucks?"

Little Timmy was walking down the sidewalk one day and passed an old man sitting on his front porch rocking back and forth in his rocking chair.

The old man said, "Whatcha got there, son?"

Timmy said, "Got me some chicken wire."

"Whatcha gonna do with that chicken wire, son?" asked the old man.

"Gonna catch me some chickens!" said Timmy.

"You can't catch chickens with chicken wire!" said the oldster.

Timmy just shrugged his shoulders and walked on down the street.

About a half hour later, Timmy came back, again passing the old man's front porch . . . with three chickens entangled in the chicken wire! The old man couldn't believe his eyes. About a half hour after this, Timmy was walking past the old man's porch for a third time.

"Whatcha got now, son?"

"Got me some duct tape."

"And whatcha gonna do with that duct tape?" the old man asked.

"Gonna catch me some ducks!"

"You can't catch ducks with duct tape!" said the old man.

Timmy just shrugged his shoulders and kept on walking. About a half hour later, back comes Timmy with three ducks tangled in the duct tape. Again, the old man rubbed his eyes in disbelief. About a half hour later, Timmy was again passing the porch.

"Whatcha got now, son?" asked the old man.

Timmy said, "Got me some pussy willow."

The old man said, "Wait right there a minute. I'm going with you!"

An attractive woman from New York was driving through a remote part of Texas when her car broke down. An Indian on horseback came along and offered her a ride to a nearby town.

She climbed up behind him on the horse and they rode off. The ride was uneventful except that every few minutes the Indian let out a whoop so loud that it echoed from the surrounding hills.

When they arrived in town, he let her off at the local service station, yelled one final "Yahoo," and rode off.

"What did you do to get that Indian so excited?" asked the service-station attendant.

"Nothing," shrugged the woman, "I merely sat behind him on the horse, put my arms around his waist, and held on to his saddle horn so I wouldn't fall off."

"Lady," the attendant said, "Indians ride bareback . . ."

Men wake up looking like they did when they went to bed. Women deteriorate overnight.

To: Management
From: The Penis
Re: Compensation

The Penis requests a promotion and a raise for the following reasons:

6

- Has to work hard
- Has to work at great depths
- Has to work upside down
- Has no ventilation or air-conditioned environment at work
- Has to work in a highly humid environment
- Has to work at high temperatures
- Does not get weekends and holidays off
- Does not get time off after extra hours of work
- Has a hazardous work environment that often causes occupation-related sickness

To: The Penis
From: Management
Re: Compensation

Request for a promotion and a raise denied for the following reasons:

- Does not work eight hours per shift
- Does not answer immediately to all requests
- After a short period of activity, falls asleep at work
- Shows no fidelity to the workplace
- Retires too early
- Does not work at all unless pushed from behind
- Does not leave the workplace clean after finishing work
- Sometimes leaves work early

An older man and a young woman go to visit a sex therapist. They both complain of a lack of enjoyment and ask if the therapist would watch what they're doing and offer some pointers. He agrees, and they go at it in his office. In the end, he says it looks like they're both doing a great job. They pay him his fifty-dollar fee and leave.

The next week, they're back in the office, doing it in front of him. Again, he says it looks great and collects his fifty dollars.

The third week, the counselor asks, "You two don't seem to have any sexual problems. Why do you keep coming back?"

The man answers, "This is my secretary, and your rates are cheaper than the Holiday Inn's."

Q: WHAT'S THE DIFFERENCE BETWEEN YOUR PAYCHECK AND YOUR PENIS?
A: You can always find a woman to blow your paycheck.

An elderly couple had been dating for some time and decided it was finally time to marry.

Before the wedding, they embarked on a long conversation regarding how their marriage might work. They discussed finances, living arrangements, and so on. Finally, the old man decided it was time to broach the subject of their sexual relationship.

"How do you feel about sex?" he asked hopefully.

"Well, I'd have to say I like it infrequently," she responded.

8

The old guy frowned, then his eyes brightened as he asked, "Was that one word or two?"

A blonde, a brunette, and a redhead all enter a swim meet. The starting gun goes off, and the redhead quickly captures first, with the brunette coming in second. An hour later, the blonde emerges from the pool and complains to the judges that while she was doing the breaststroke, the others were using their arms.

Some signs that your son is too old for breast-feeding:

He can open your wife's blouse by himself, with one hand.

While sucking on one breast, he fondles the other.

He keeps slipping dollar bills in your wife's belt.

He uses her milk as creamer for his coffee.

After each feeding, he has a smoke.

He frequently invites his friends over for dinner.

Number 67 on the List of Things a Man Should *Not* Say During Sex:
"On second thought, let's turn off the lights."

A young man goes into a drugstore to buy condoms for the first time. The pharmacist senses his uneasiness and goes over to help.

"How thick are you?" she asks.

"What do you mean?" says the young man.

She holds out one finger. "Are you this thick?"

"No, I'm thicker than that."

She holds out two fingers.

"I'm thicker than that," he says again.

She holds out three fingers.

"I'm about that thick."

She sticks her fingers in her mouth and says, "Okay. You're a medium."

A visiting professor at the University of Arkansas is giving a lecture on the supernatural.

To get a feel for his audience, he asks, "How many people here believe in ghosts?"

About ninety students raise their hands.

"Well, that's a good start," says the professor. "Out of those of you who believe in ghosts, do any of you think you've ever seen a ghost?"

About forty students raise their hands.

"That's really good," continues the professor. "I'm really glad you take this seriously. Has anyone here ever talked to a ghost?"

Fifteen students raise their hands.

"That's a great response," remarks the impressed professor. "Has anyone here ever touched a ghost?"

Three students raise their hands.

"That's fantastic. But let me ask you one question further . . . Have any of you ever made love to a ghost?" asks the professor.

One student in the back raises his hand.

The professor is astonished.

He takes off his glasses, takes a step back, and says, "Son, all the years I've been giving this lecture, no one has ever claimed to have slept with a ghost. You've got to come up here and tell us about your experience."

The student replies with a nod and begins to make his way up to the podium.

The professor asks, "Well, tell us what it's like to have sex with a ghost."

The student replies, "Ghost? Dang, I thought you said 'goats.' "

Two boys are playing catch with a football in Central Park when one is attacked by a rabid pit bull. Thinking quickly, the other boy rips a board from a nearby fence, wedges it down the dog's collar, and gives it a hard twist, breaking the dog's neck. A reporter who was walking by witnesses the incident and rushes over to interview the boy. "Young Giants Fan Saves Friend from Vicious Animal," he starts writing in his notebook.

"But I'm not a Giants fan," the little hero says.

"Sorry, since we are in New York, I just assumed you were," says the reporter, and starts again. "Little Jets Fan Rescues Friend from Horrific Attack," he now writes in his notebook.

"I'm not a Jets fan either," the boy says.

"I assumed everyone in New York was either for the Giants or Jets. What team do you root for?" the reporter asks.

"I'm a Cowboys fan," the child says.

The reporter starts a new sheet in his notebook and writes, "Little Redneck Maniac Kills Beloved Family Pet."

Two men are sitting next to each other in an Irish-style pub in New York City. They both order pints of Guinness. One of them turns to the other and says "So where are you from, then?"

"I'm from Ireland."

"Me, too! I'll drink to that." They both finish their pints and order two more.

"Where in Ireland are you from?"

"Dublin."

"Me, too! I'll drink to that." They both finish their pints and order two more.

"Where in Dublin are you from?"

"The East Side."

"The East Side? Me, too! What a coincidence! I'll drink to that!" They both finish their pints and order two more.

"Where on the East Side are you from?"

"McDonagh Street."

"Me, too! This is incredible! I'll drink to that."

As the bartender pours them another two pints, another customer at the bar says to him, "That's amazing! I can't believe they're from the same street in Dublin. What's going on?"

"Oh, it's nothing amazing," says the bartender. "It's just the Shannahan twins getting sloshed again."

Because Jim works hard at the plant and spends most evenings bowling or playing basketball at the gym, his wife thinks he is pushing himself too hard. So for his birthday, she takes him to a local strip club.

The doorman at the club greets them and says, "Hey, Jim! How ya doin'?" His wife is puzzled and asks if he's been to this club before.

"Oh no," says Jim. "He's on my bowling team."

When they are seated, a waitress asks Jim if he'd like his usual Budweiser.

His wife is becoming uncomfortable and says, "You must come here a lot for that woman to know you drink Budweiser."

"No, honey, she's in the Ladies Bowling League. We share lanes with them."

A stripper comes over to their table and throws her arms around Jim. "Hi, Jimmy," she says, "want your usual table dance?"

Jim's wife, now furious, grabs her purse and storms out of the club. Jim follows and spots her getting into a cab. Before she can slam the door, he jumps in beside her and she starts screaming at him. The cabbie turns his head and says, "Looks like you picked up a real doozy this time, Jim!"

Two golfers are on the first tee, and the first guy has spent at least five minutes lining up his tee shot.

"Sorry to take so long, but my wife is up there watching from the clubhouse, so this shot has to be perfect," he explains.

"Oh, for Christ's sake," the second says. "You'll never hit her from here."

There once was a rural minister who was raising three daughters on his own. He was very concerned about their well-being and always did his best to watch out for them. As they entered their late teens, the girls began dating, and on this particular evening, all three of them were going out. This was the first time this had occurred. It was the minister's custom to greet the young suitor at the door holding his shotgun, not to menace or threaten, but merely to ensure that the young man knew who was boss.

The doorbell rang and the first of the boys arrived. Father answered the door and the boy said, "Hi, my name's Joe, I'm here for Flo. We're going to the show; is she ready to go?"

The father looked him over and sent the kids on their way.

The next lad arrived and said, "My name's Eddie, I'm here for Betty, we're gonna get some spaghetti; is she ready?"

Father felt this one was okay, too, so off the two kids went.

The last young man arrived and the minister opened the door. The boy started off, "Hi, my name's Chuck . . ." and the father shot him.

An Irishman, an American, and a Scotsman go into a pub and each orders a pint of Guinness. Just as the bartender hands them over, three flies buzz down and one lands in each of the pints.

The American looks disgusted, pushes his pint away, and demands another pint.

The Scotsman picks out the fly, shrugs, and takes a long swallow.

The Irishman reaches into the glass, pinches the fly between his fingers, and shakes him while yelling, "Spit it out, ya bastard! Spit it out!"

There was a guy who was struggling to decide what to wear to a fancy costume party. Then he had a bright idea and went to the party. When the host answered the door, he found the guy standing there with no shirt and no socks on.

"What the hell are you supposed to be?" asked the host.

"A premature ejaculation," said the man. "I just came in my pants!"

The host showed him inside and introduced him to a man who was naked except for a piece of bread. The piece of bread had a hole in it, through which the man had pushed his member.

"What are you dressed as?" asked the first guy.

"Coming through the Rye," said the second.

A cowboy is captured by Indians, who plan to scalp him. The chief tells him he will try to grant three of the cowboy's last requests.

The cowboy says his first wish is to say good-bye to his horse and his second is to set him free.

"Bring him his horse," the chief says. The cowboy strokes the horse's mane, whispers in his ear, and then sends him on his way into the sunset.

The cowboy says he would like to mull over his final request, and the chief gives him until sunset.

Just as the sun begins to dip below the mountains a few hours later, the cowboy hears hooves approaching and looks to the distance. Sure enough, here comes his horse—with a beautiful brunette in the saddle.

"Is this part of your final request?" the chief asks.

"Uh, no," the cowboy says. "For my final request, I would like to say good-bye to my horse once more."

"Very well," the chief says.

This time, the cowboy leans into his horse and whispers: "You idiot! I said, 'Posse! Posse!' "

One day a man took his father to a nursing home. The next day, the son returned and his father greeted him with a big smile.

"You know, son, I think I'm going to like it here. When I got here yesterday, they showed me to my room, and I stretched out on the bed and got a big hard-on, and right then a beautiful young nurse came into the room and gave me the best sex I've had in thirty years!"

His son said, "That's great, Dad! I'll come back again tomorrow."

So the next day the man returned to check on his father. His dad said, "Son, I can't stay in this place for another minute. You've got to get me the hell out of here now!"

His son said, "But, Dad, I thought you liked it here. What happened?"

His dad said, "This morning an orderly came in to give me a bath. Well, I fell down and he had his way with me right there on the floor. It was terrible! Now get me out of here!"

His son said, "But, Dad, you always taught me to take the bad with the good."

"True," the father said. "But I'm lucky if I get a hard-on once a month. I fall down at least five or six times a day!"

The doctor says to his patient: "I have good news and bad news, Mr. Henderson. The bad news is you are dying, and you have only three months to live."

"Jesus," the patient says. "That's terrible. What's the good news?"

"Do you see that gorgeous blonde in the reception area?" says the doctor, pointing to the well-built nurse outside his office door. "I'm fucking her."

Q: HOW DID THE BLONDE DIE ICE FISHING?
A: A puck hit her in the head.

A man and a wife are stranded on a desert island for years before another raft washes ashore, bearing a lone man. The couple is happy for the company and intrigued by the presence of a third person, but they both say they care too much about their marriage to share each other with anyone else. Meanwhile, they are elated to have a third person help with watchtower duty, looking for passing ships.

During the new man's first shift in the tower, he looks down at the couple as they arrange rocks for the night's fire.

"Hey!" he calls out. "No fucking!"

"We're not fucking!" the husband shouts back.

On the man's second shift, he again looks down at the husband and wife—this time, they're cleaning fish—and shouts, "Hey! No fucking!"

"But we're not," the husband yells back.

The next day, the husband climbs the tower for his shift. He looks down at his wife and the man tending to their chores.

"I'll be," he says to himself. "From up here, it *does* look like they're fucking."

Q: WHY DO WOMEN TAKE THE PILL?
A: To remember what day it is.

A woman walks into the store and purchases a small box of detergent, one bar of soap, three single-size yogurts, two oranges, and a stick of women's deodorant.

The cashier says, "Oh, you must be single."

18

"Gee, you think so?" says the woman. "I guess you're a genius because you can tell that from what I'm buying."

"No," says the cashier. "I can tell because you're so ugly."

Three nuns were whispering at lunch in the convent. The first nun said, "I was cleaning in Father's room the other day and do you know what I found? A bunch of pornographic magazines."

"What did you do?" the other two nuns wanted to know.

"Well, of course I threw them in the trash," said the first.

The second nun said, "Well, I can top that. I was in Father's room putting away the laundry and I found a bunch of condoms!"

"Oh my!" gasped the first nun. "What did you do?"

"I poked holes in all of them!" she replied.

Just then, the third nun fainted.

**Q:** WHY DID THE BLONDE FAIL HER DRIVER'S TEST?
**A:** The front seat scared her.

Have you heard about the woman who was so rank, she put ice cubes down her pants to keep the crabs fresh?

A man was walking along a California beach and stumbled across an old lamp. He picked it up and rubbed it and out popped a genie!

The genie said, "I will grant you one wish."

The man sat down on the beach and thought about it for a while. Then he said, "I've always wanted to go to Hawaii, but I'm afraid of flying and I get very seasick on ships. Could you build me a bridge to Hawaii so that I can drive there to visit?"

The genie laughed and said, "That's impossible! Think of the logistics! How would the supports ever reach the bottom of the Pacific? Think of the concrete, the steel, the shipping hazards. No. Think of another wish."

The man tried to think of another wish. Finally, he said, "I've been married and divorced several times. My wives always said that I don't care and that I'm insensitive. So, I wish that I could understand women, know exactly what they mean when they're talking, and know how to answer their questions without getting into trouble."

The genie said, "You want that bridge to be two lanes or four?"

Then there was the girl who was so stupid, they had to burn down the school to get her out of second grade.

This man is walking down the beach and hears someone weeping. He stops and sees a woman without any arms or legs crying beside an ocean pool.

He asks, "What's the problem?"

"I've never been hugged before," she answers.

Well, this is a nice guy, so he walks over and gives her a hug. Half an hour later, he is going back to his car and hears her crying again.

He asks, "Now what's wrong?"

She says, "I've been thinking about it, and I realize I've never been kissed before."

The guy thinks what's the harm in giving her a kiss to make her feel better? He kneels down and gives her a kiss. At his car, he finds that he left his keys behind, so he goes back to the girl to find them, and sure enough, there she is crying again.

"Now what's wrong?" he asks.

She says, "I've never made love with anyone before."

The guy picks her up, throws her into the ocean, and says, "Now you're fucked."

When the collection plate came to young Michael, he took three dollars in bills. The priest, watching from the altar, took note, but decided to ignore it this once. But the next week, Michael stole five dollars. The next week, seven.

Furious, the priest confronted Michael after the service, demanding to know why he would steal from the church. Ashamed, Michael answered: "I'm sorry, Father. It was for a blow job."

The priest had never heard that term before, but chastised Michael anyway, then went to see Sister Agnes.

"Sister," the priest asked the nun, "what is a blow job?"

"Fifteen dollars," she replied.

Mrs. Smith goes to the doctor for a physical exam.

After an hour or so, the doctor looks at her and says, "Mrs. Smith, overall you are very healthy for a forty-five-year-old. There is, however, one problem. You are forty pounds overweight and bordering on obesity. I strongly suggest that you diet now to save any complications in your later years."

She looks sternly at him and replies, "I really think I'd like a second opinion, Doctor."

"Fine," he says. "You're fucking ugly, too!"

Q: WHAT'S THE DIFFERENCE BETWEEN A WOMAN JOGGING AND A SEWING MACHINE?
A: A sewing machine only has one bobbin.

Two parents take their son on vacation and go to a nude beach. The father decides to take a walk on the beach and the son goes to play in the water. Shortly thereafter, the boy runs to his mother and says, "Mommy, I saw some ladies with boobies a lot bigger than yours!"

The mother cleverly replies, "The bigger they are, the dumber they are!"

With that, the little boy runs back into the water and continues to play. Several minutes later, though, he runs back to his mother and says, "Mommy, I saw some men with pee-pees a lot bigger than Daddy's!"

"The bigger they are, the dumber they are!" she replies.

With that, the little boy runs back into the water and continues to play. Several minutes later, he runs back to his mother and says, "Mommy, I just saw Daddy talking to the dumbest lady I ever saw, and the more he talked, the dumber he got!"

The definition of trust: receiving a cannibal's first blow job.

A woman went to see a therapist and said, "I've got a big problem, Doctor. Every time we're in bed and my husband climaxes, he lets out this very loud yell."

"That's completely natural," the therapist said. "A lot of people make noise during sex. What's the problem?"

"The problem," she complained, "is that it wakes me up."

Q: WHAT'S THE EASIEST WAY TO GET A GREAT BLOW JOB FROM YOUR WIFE?
A: Steal fifty dollars from her purse.

There was a virgin who was going out on a date for the first time and was so concerned about it that she talked to her mother.

So the mother says, "Sit here and let me tell you about young boys. He is going to try to kiss you, and you are going to like that, but don't let him do it. He is going to try to feel your breasts, and you are going to like that, but don't let him do it. He is going to try to put his hand between your legs, you are going to like that, too, but don't let him do it. Most important, he is going to try to get on top of you and have his way with you. You are going to like that, but don't let him do it, because it will disgrace the family."

With that bit of advice, the daughter went on her date and could not wait to tell her mother about it. So, the next day she told her mother that her date went just as her mother predicted.

Then she said, "Mother, I didn't let him disgrace the family. When he tried, I turned over, got on top of him, and disgraced *his* family."

**WOMAN TO HER DENTIST:** I'd rather give birth than get my tooth pulled.

**DENTIST:** Well, make up your mind so I know how much gas to use.

A woman arrived home after a long shopping trip and was horrified to find her husband in bed with a gorgeous young girl. Just as she was about to storm out of the house, her husband jumped up and stopped her with this story.

"Before you leave, I want you to hear how this all came about. Driving home, I saw this girl, looking poor and tired, and I offered her a ride," he said. "She was hungry, so I brought her home and fed her some of the roast you had forgotten about in the refrigerator. Her shoes were worn out, so I gave her a pair of your shoes you no longer wear because they are out of style. She was cold, so I gave her that new birthday sweater you never wore because you didn't like the color. Her slacks were worn, so I gave her a pair of yours that you don't fit into anymore. Then, as she was about to leave the house, she paused and asked, 'Is there anything else that your wife doesn't use anymore?' And so, here we are!"

A naive man was a little clueless on his wedding night, so he called his mother for advice. "Take that thing you always play with," she said, "and stick it where she pees."

So he grabbed his bowling ball and threw it in the toilet.

Q: WHAT DO YOU CALL A MAN WHO DOESN'T EXPECT A WOMAN TO HAVE SEX ON THE FIRST DATE?
A: Gay.

Three women were on an airplane—a white woman, an Asian, and an African—when suddenly the captain announced, "Please prepare for a crash landing."

The first lady put on all her jewelry. Surprised by this, the other two asked what she was doing.

The first lady replied, "When they come to rescue us, they will see that I am rich and will rescue me first."

The second woman, not wanting to be left behind, began to take off her top and bra.

"Why are you doing that?" the others asked.

"When they come to rescue us, they'll see my great tits and will take me first."

The third lady, not wanting to be outdone, took off her pants and panties.

"Why are you doing that?" the other ladies asked.

"Well," she said, "they always search for the black box first, don't they?"

MAN NO. 1: My wife came out of the kitchen all last night nagging me.

MAN NO. 2: That's your fault. You made her chain too long.

A cop saw a car weaving all over the road and pulled it over. He walked up to the car and saw a nice-looking red-head behind the wheel. There was a strong liquor smell all over the car.

"I'm going to give you a Breathalyzer test," he said. "That will show whether or not you are under the influence of alcohol."

She blew up the balloon and he walked it back to the police car. After a couple of minutes, he returned to her car.

"It looks like you've had a couple of stiff ones," he said.

"You mean it shows that, too?" she replied.

A woman stood by her husband's bedside for months as he slipped in and out of a coma. When he regained consciousness for a few minutes after months of struggling to communicate, he motioned for his wife to come nearer.

"What is it, my dearest?" she asked in a whisper.

"Life has been difficult, and you have been with me through all the bad times," he said. "When I got fired, you went to work to pay the bills. When my business failed, you were there. When my parents died, you were by my side. When we lost the house, you gave me support. When my health started failing, you were still by my side. You know what?"

"What, dear?" she asked gently.

"You must be bad luck."

A woman had been away for two days in another town. When she returned, her little boy greeted her by saying, "Mommy, guess what! Yesterday I was playing in the closet in your bedroom and Daddy came into the room with the lady next door and they got undressed and got into your bed and then Daddy got on top of her—"

The woman held up her hand. "Don't say another word. Wait till your father comes home, and then I want you to tell him exactly what you just told me."

Later, when the father walked into the house, his wife said, "I'm leaving you. I'm packing now and then I'm going for good."

"Why?" asked the startled father.

"Go ahead, Timmy," she said. "Tell Daddy just what you told me."

"Well," Timmy said, "I was playing in your bedroom closet and Daddy came upstairs with the lady next door and they got undressed and got into bed and Daddy got on top of her and then they did just what you did with Uncle John when Daddy was away last summer."

Q: WHAT, EXACTLY, ARE CATS?

1. Cats do what they want, when they want.

2. They never listen.

3. They are not predictable.

4. They whine when they are not happy.

5. When you want to play, they want to be left alone.

6. When you want to be alone, they want to play.

7. They expect you to cater to their every whim.

8. They're moody.

9. They leave their hair everywhere.

10. They drive you nuts.

A: Cats are small women in fur coats.

An old lady is rocking away the last of her days on her front porch, reflecting on her long life, when suddenly her fairy godmother appears in front of her and grants her three wishes.

"Well, now," says the old lady, "I guess I would like to be really, really rich." Just like that, her rocking chair turns to solid gold.

She smiles and says, "Gee, I guess I wouldn't mind being a young, beautiful princess." Instantly, she turns into a beautiful young woman.

"And for your third wish?" asks the fairy godmother. Just then the old woman's cat wanders across the porch in front of them.

"Ooh . . . can you change him into a handsome prince?" she asks. As soon as she speaks, there before her stands a young man more handsome than anyone could possibly imagine. She stares at him, smitten.

With a smile that makes her knees weak, he strolls across the porch and whispers in her ear, "Bet you're sorry you had me neutered!"

A man and a woman who have never met before find themselves in the same sleeping car on a train.

After the initial embarrassment, they both go to sleep, the woman on the top bunk, the man on the lower.

In the middle of the night the woman leans over, wakes the man, and says, "I'm sorry to bother you, but I'm awfully cold and I was wondering if you could possibly get me another blanket."

The man leans out and, with a glint in his eye, says,

"I've got a better idea. Just for tonight, why don't we pretend that we're married?"

The woman thinks for a moment. "Why not?" she giggles.

"Great," he replies. "Get your own damn blanket!"

Miss Jessica had just returned from her big trip to New York City and was having some refreshments on the front porch of her daddy's mansion with her Southern-belle friends. She told them the stories of her trip as they stared spellbound.

"You just wouldn't believe what they have there in New York City," she said. "They have men there who kiss other men on the lips."

Miss Jessica's friends fanned themselves and said, "Oh, Lordy!"

"They call them homosexuals," proclaimed Miss Jessica.

"Oh, Lordy," said the girls, fanning themselves.

"They also have women there in New York City who kiss other women on the lips!"

"Oh, Lordy," exclaimed the girls. "What do they call them?"

"They call them lesbians," said Miss Jessica.

"They also have men who kiss women between the legs," sighed Miss Jessica.

"Oh, Lordy," exclaimed the girls, sitting on the edge of their chairs and fanning themselves even faster. "What do they call a man like that?" they asked in unison.

Miss Jessica leaned forward and said in a hush, "Why, when I caught my breath, I called him Precious."

A stunning woman driving a BMW pulls out in front of a man in a pickup truck. The result is a bad collision which ends with both vehicles upside down. Amazingly, both drivers emerge unscathed.

After they crawl out of their cars, the woman says, "Wow, just look at our cars! There's nothing left, but fortunately we aren't hurt. This must be a sign from God that we should meet and be friends and live together in peace for the rest of our days."

Flattered, the man replies, "Oh yes, I agree with you completely!"

"This must indeed be a sign from God!" the woman continues. "And look at this, here's another miracle. My car is completely demolished, but this bottle of vodka didn't break. Surely God wants us to drink this vodka and celebrate our good fortune."

She hands the bottle to the man. He nods his head in agreement, opens it and drinks six belts, and then hands it back to the woman. The woman takes the bottle, immediately puts the cap back on, and hands it back to the man.

The man asks, "Aren't you having any?"

The woman replies, "No. On second thought, I think I'll just wait for the police . . ."

Three women were sitting around throwing back a few drinks and talking about their sex lives. May said, "I call my husband the dentist because nobody can drill like he does."

Joanne giggled and confessed, "I call my husband the miner because of his incredible shaft."

Kathy quietly sipped her whiskey until Joanne finally asked, "Well, what do you call your boyfriend?"

Kathy frowned and said, "The postman."

"Why the postman?" asked Joanne.

"Because, he always delivers late and half the time it's in the wrong box."

🃏

**Q:** WHAT'S THE DIFFERENCE BETWEEN A GIRLFRIEND AND A WIFE?
**A:** About forty-five pounds.

🃏

There were three prostitutes living together: a grand-mother, a mother, and a daughter. One night the daughter came home looking very down.

"How did you get on tonight, dear?" asked her mother.

"Not too good," replied the daughter. "I only got ten dollars for a blow job."

"Wow!" said the mother. "In my day we only got a dollar for a blow job!"

"Good God!" said the grandmother. "In my day we were just glad to get something warm in our stomachs!"

🃏

A model went to the appliance-store sale and found a bargain. "I would like to buy this TV," she told the salesman.

"Sorry, we don't sell to models," he replied.

She hurried home and dyed her hair black, then came back and again told the salesman, "I would like to buy this TV."

"Sorry, we don't sell to models," he replied.

"Darn," she thought. "He recognized me."

She went for a complete disguise this time—haircut and new color, new outfit, big sunglasses—and then waited a few days before she again approached the salesman. "I would like to buy this TV," she said when she saw him again.

"Sorry, we don't sell to models," he replied.

Frustrated, she exclaimed, "How do you know I'm a model?"

"Because that's not a TV," he replied. "It's a microwave."

A man and woman had been married for some time when the woman began to question her husband.

"I know you've been with a lot of woman before," she said. "How many were there?"

The husband replied, "Look, I don't want to upset you, but there were more than a couple of women. Let's just leave it at that."

The wife continued to plead. Finally, her husband gave in.

"Let's see," he said. "There was one, two, three, four, five, six, you, eight, nine . . ."

Q: HOW CAN YOU TELL IF A WOMAN HAS BEEN USING THE COMPUTER?

**A:** There's Wite-Out all over the screen.

Harry left on a two-day business trip to Chicago. He was only a few blocks away from his house on the way to the airport when he realized he'd left his plane ticket on top of the dresser. He turned around and headed back to the house. He entered the front door and walked into the kitchen, where he saw his wife washing the breakfast dishes, wearing her skimpiest negligee. She looked so good that he tiptoed up behind her, reached out, and squeezed her left tit.

"Leave only one quart of milk," she said. "Harry won't be here for breakfast tomorrow."

**Q:** WHAT'S A BLONDE'S FAVORITE NURSERY RHYME?
**A:** "Humpme. Dumpme."

A woman asks her husband if he'd like some breakfast. "Bacon and eggs, perhaps a slice of toast? Maybe a fruit salad and some crepes, and a pot of fresh coffee?" He declines.

"It's this Viagra," he says. "It's really taken the edge off my appetite."

At lunchtime, she asks if he would like something. "A bowl of homemade soup, maybe, with a cheese sandwich? Or how about a plate of snacks and a glass of milk?" Again he declines.

"No, thanks. It's this Viagra," he says. "It's really taken the edge off my appetite."

At dinnertime, she asks if he wants anything to eat, offering to go to the café and buy him a burger supper. "Or would you rather I make you a pizza from scratch? Or how about a tasty stir-fry? That'll only take a couple of minutes . . ." Once more, he declines.

"Thanks, but it's this Viagra. It's really taken the edge off my appetite."

"Well then," she says, "would you mind getting off me? I'm STARVING!"

Two women are walking down the road when one says, "Look at that dog with one eye!"

The second woman covers one of her eyes and says, "Where?"

When her husband passed away, the wife put the usual death notice in the newspaper, but added that he had died of gonorrhea. When the newspaper came out, a friend of the family phoned and complained.

"You know very well that he died of diarrhea, not gonorrhea," he said.

"Yes, I know he died of diarrhea," replied the widow. "But I thought it would be better to remember him for his sex life than for being the big shit that he really was."

It was a really hot day and a woman decided she would go buy a Coke. She went to the Coke machine and put her money in, and a Coke came out. So she kept putting money in the machine and watching the Cokes come out. Since it was a hot day, a line formed behind her. Finally, the man immediately behind her said, "Will you hurry up. We're all hot and thirsty!"

The woman turned around and said, "No way. I'm still winning."

A woman went to her doctor for a checkup. When asked how she got the bruises on her thighs, she explained that she had gotten them from sex. The doctor suggested that she change positions until the bruises healed.

"Oh, Doctor, I can't," she replied. "My dog's breath is awful!"

Two women are walking down the street when one of them looks down and finds a mirror. She picks it up and looks into it.

"WOW! I know this person. I've seen her before."

The other woman takes the mirror and looks at it.

"Of course you do," she sneers. "That's me."

One day God and Adam were walking in the Garden of Eden, and God told Adam that it was time to propagate the human species on the earth.

"Adam, you can start by kissing Eve."

Adam looked puzzled at God and said, "Lord, what is a kiss?"

God explained, and then Adam took Eve behind a tree and kissed her.

A while later, Adam returned with a big smile and said, "Lord! That was great! What's next?"

"Adam, I now want you to caress Eve."

Puzzled, Adam asked, "Lord, what is a caress?"

God explained, and then Adam took Eve behind the tree and caressed her.

A while later, Adam returned with a big smile and said, "Lord that was even better than a kiss! What's next?"

"I now want you to have sex with Eve."

"Lord, what is sex?" asked Adam.

God explained, and then Adam took Eve behind the tree once more.

A few seconds later, Adam returned and asked, "Lord, what is a headache?"

Q: **WHAT GOES VROOM-SKREECH-VROOM-SKREECH-VROOM?**
A: A woman driving through a flashing red light.

Q: **WHY DID THE WOMAN GET SO EXCITED AFTER SHE FINISHED HER JIGSAW PUZZLE IN ONLY SIX MONTHS?**
A: Because on the box it said, "From 2 to 4 years."

Annoyed by a professor of history who liked to tell off-color stories during class, a group of female students decided that the next time he started to tell one, they would all rise and leave the room in protest. The professor got wind of their scheme just before class the following day, however, so he bided his time. Then, halfway through the lecture, he began.

"They say there is quite a shortage of prostitutes in France," he said.

The girls looked at one another, arose, and started for the door.

"Ladies, please," said the professor with a smile. "The next plane doesn't leave till tomorrow afternoon."

The definition of a perfect woman, Part I: A deaf-and-dumb blond nymphomaniac whose father owns a liquor store.

The definition of a perfect woman, Part II: A deaf-and-dumb blond nymphomaniac who is three feet tall and has a flat head to rest your beer on.

Q: WHAT DID THE BLOND OWL SAY?
A: Huh? Huh?

Q: WHY WAS THE BLONDE SNORTING EQUAL?

**A:** She wanted to use diet Coke.

A woman says to her psychotherapist, "My sex life stinks."

The therapist says, "Do you ever watch your husband's face when you're having sex?"

She says, "Once, and I saw rage."

The therapist asks, "Why would he be angry during sex?"

The woman says, "Because he was looking through the window at us."

**Q:** HOW DO YOU GET A ONE-ARMED BLONDE OUT OF A TREE?
**A:** Wave to her.

**Q:** HOW DO YOU CONFUSE A BLONDE FOR ABOUT AN HOUR?
**A:** Give her a bag of M&Ms and tell her to put them in alphabetical order.

A model walks into the hairdresser with headphones on. She asks the woman working there for a haircut. The model sits down in the chair. The woman takes the model's headphones off and cuts her hair. At the end, the woman starts to ask how she likes her hair, but to her surprise, the model is dead! The woman picks up the headphones and listens. She hears: "Breathe in . . . breathe out . . . breathe in . . . breathe out."

The headmistress at an exclusive girls' school was lecturing her students on sexual morality.

"We live today in very difficult times for young people. In moments of temptation," she says, "ask yourself just one question: Is an hour of pleasure worth a lifetime of shame?"

A girl in the back of the room rises and says, "Excuse me, but how do you make it last an hour?"

Q: WHY DID THE WOMAN PUT LIPSTICK ON HER FOREHEAD?

A: She was trying to make up her mind.

A cop stops a blonde who is driving along a highway.

"Miss, may I see your driver's license please?" he asks.

"Driver's license? What's that?" she replies.

"It's a little card with your picture on it," he says.

"Oh, duh! Here it is," she says, handing him her license.

"May I have your car insurance?" he asks next.

"What's that?" she says.

"It's a document that says you are allowed to drive the car," he answers.

"Oh this? Duh! Here you go," she says.

The cop then takes his dick out of his pants.

"Oh no," says the blonde. "Not another Breathalyzer test!"

A man and his wife visiting the zoo wander over to the gorilla cage. It's late and they are the only ones there.

"Honey," the man says, "take off your clothes and see if it gets the gorilla excited."

She protests at first, but is curious, so eventually she agrees. The gorilla seems to be drooling as he watches, and by the end is grunting and jumping up and down in the cage. Naked, the woman smiles at her husband, who quickly unlocks the cage and throws his wife in with the frenzied ape.

"Now tell *him* you have a headache."

A guy marries a woman. Unfortunately, his dick is so small that he can't have sex with her and secretly uses a pickle instead. This goes on for seven years. One night his wife finally suspects that something is wrong. When they start to have sex, she throws the covers off the bed, turns on the lights, and sees the pickle.

"What the hell is that? Are you using a pickle on me?

For seven years you have been doing that, you piece of shit."

So the man says, "Keep quiet! It's been seven years, and I never asked where the hell those kids came from!"

Three blondes are training to be police officers. Their sergeant holds up a mug shot.

"This is your suspect," he says. "How would you recognize him later?"

"He only has one eye!" says the first blonde.

"That's because this is a profile shot," explains the sergeant.

"He only has one ear!" says the second blonde.

"That's because this is a sideways photo," replies the sergeant.

"He's wearing contact lenses," says the third blonde.

"Actually, this guy does wear contact lenses," answers the sergeant. "How can you tell?"

"How could a guy with one ear and one eye wear regular glasses?" answers the third blonde.

One dismal rainy night, a taxi driver spotted an arm waving from the shadows of an alley halfway down the block. Even before he rolled to a stop at the curb, a figure leaped into the cab and slammed the door. Checking his rearview mirror as he pulled away, he was startled to see a dripping-wet, naked woman sitting in the backseat.

"Where to?" he stammered.

"Union Station," answered the woman.

"You got it," he said, taking another long glance in the mirror.

The woman caught him staring at her and asked, "Just what the hell are you looking at, driver?"

The driver replied, "Well, ma'am, I noticed that you're completely naked, and I was just wondering how you'll pay your fare."

The woman spread her legs, put her feet up on the front seat, smiled at the driver, and said, "Does this answer your question?"

Still looking in the mirror, the cabbie asked, "Got anything smaller?"

Once upon a time there was a magic mirror that could tell when you were lying. If you were—*poof*—it would suck you in and you were gone forever. One day, an old lady, a female scientist, and a blonde walked past the mirror.

The old lady looked in it and said, "I think I'm the most beautiful woman in the world."

*Poof!* The mirror sucked her in and she was gone.

The scientist looked in and said, "I think I'm the most beautiful woman in the world."

*Poof!* The mirror sucked her in and she, too, disappeared.

The blonde looked in and said, "I think . . ."

*Poof!*

A man and his wife go to the dentist's office.

The wife says, "I want a tooth pulled. No gas or

painkillers, because we're in a hurry. Just pull the tooth as quickly as possible."

"You're a brave woman," says the dentist. "Now show me which tooth it is."

The wife turns to her husband and says: "Open your mouth and show the dentist which tooth it is, dear."

A redhead says to a model, "Look! A dead bird!" and the model looks up and says, "Where?"

Q: WHAT DO YOU CALL A MODEL WITH TWO BRAIN CELLS?
A: Pregnant.

Q: WHY ARE DUMB-BLONDE JOKES SO SHORT?
A: So other women can remember them.

A couple revisited their honeymoon hotel on their twenty-fifth anniversary. As the two of them reflected on that special evening twenty-five years before, the wife asked the husband, "When you first saw my naked body in front of you, what went through your mind?"

The husband replied, "All I wanted to do was to fuck your brains out and suck your tits dry."

Then, as the wife undressed provocatively, she asked, "What are you thinking now?"

"I was thinking that I did a pretty good job."

**Q:** WHAT HAPPENED WHEN THE BLONDE SHOT AN ARROW INTO THE AIR?

**A:** She missed.

Blonde Invention Number 367: foot-powered wheelchairs.

An elderly wife decides it's time to spice up her sex life with her husband. At bedtime that night, she waits in their closet wearing only a red satin cape. When she hears him get into bed, she bursts out of the closet and announces: "Super Pussy!"

The man looks up and says, "I think I'll have the soup."

A blonde goes for a job interview. The human-resources coordinator starts with some basic information.

"So, miss, can you tell us your age, please?"

The model counts carefully on her fingers for about thirty seconds before replying, "Twenty-two."

The interviewer tries another straightforward one to break the ice.

"And can you tell us your height, please?"

The young lady stands up and pulls out a measuring tape from her handbag. She then traps one end under her foot and extends the tape to the top of her head. She checks the measurement and announces, "Five foot two!"

This isn't looking good, so the interviewer goes for the real basics.

"And, just to confirm for our records, your name please?"

The blonde bobs her head from side to side for about twenty seconds, mouthing something silently to herself, before replying, "Mandy!"

The interviewer is completely baffled at this point, so he asks, "Just out of curiosity, miss. We can understand your counting on your fingers to work out your age, and the measuring tape for your height is obvious, but what were you doing when we asked you your name?"

"I was just running through 'Happy birthday to you, happy birthday to you . . .' " she replies.

Q: WHY DID THE BLONDE STOP USING THE PILL?
A: Because it kept falling out.

A nurse was walking down the hospital corridor when her supervisor saw her. Her hair was unkempt, her uniform looked like she had slept in it, and one of her breasts was hanging out of the open front of her blouse. Her supervisor was stunned.

"Miss Jennings! How can you go around the hospital looking like a bum and with your breast exposed!" the supervisor yelled.

"Oh," said the nurse as she stuffed her breast into her

uniform. "It's those darn interns! They *never* put anything back when they're done using it!"

**Q:** WHAT ARE THE FEMALE REINDEER DOING WHILE SANTA AND HIS TEAM DELIVER PRESENTS ON CHRISTMAS EVE?
**A:** Wandering the mall, blowing a few bucks.

**Q:** HOW CAN YOU TELL WHEN A PARTICULARLY DUMB WOMAN HAS BEEN BAKING CHOCOLATE CHIP COOKIES?
**A:** There are M&M shells all over the floor.

On the eve of his wedding night, a young man went to his mother with the following question: "Mom, why are wedding dresses white?"

The mother looked at her son and replied, "Son, this shows the town that your bride is pure."

The son thanked his mom and went to double-check this with his father. "Dad, why are wedding dresses white?"

The father said, "All household appliances come in white."

Three men are at a bar, discussing Christmas gifts for their wives.

"I bought mine a diamond ring and a fur coat, and told

her if she doesn't like the coat, at least the ring will always sparkle."

"I bought mine a pool and a BMW, and told her if she doesn't want to swim, she can always travel in style."

"Well, I bought mine a Hoover cleaner and a dildo," the third said. "I told her if she doesn't like the vacuum cleaner, she can go fuck herself."

A man picks up his girlfriend in his new Mercedes on the way back from a golf outing. She slides in the front seat, looks down, and spies a box of tees.

"What are these for?"

"That's what we put our balls on before we drive," he answers.

"Wow," she replies, "the Germans really think of everything."

Q: WHAT'S THE DEFINITION OF A SLUT?
A: A woman who sleeps with everyone but you.

Q: WHAT IS SIX INCHES LONG, WRINKLY, HAS A BIG HEAD, AND DRIVES WOMEN WILD?
A: A hundred-dollar bill.

Q: WHY DID GOD GIVE MODELS A BIT MORE BRAINS THAN SEAGULLS?

**A:** So they wouldn't shit on statues.

**Q:** WHAT HAPPENED TO THE BLOND TAP DANCER?
**A:** She slipped off the sink and bumped her head.

A woman is lonely from all her husband's business trips, so she decides to buy a parrot. There's one for sale at a local pet shop, but the clerk warns her about it.

"This is sort of a nasty old bird," he tells her. "It used to live in a whorehouse, which is where it learned to talk."

This doesn't bother the woman, so she buys the bird and take him home. The first week, it says only one thing, "Whores for twenty bucks! Whores for twenty bucks!"

The second week, it adds another phrase. It says, "Awwk! New whores! Awwk! New whores!"

The talk is filthy, but she knows her husband will get a kick out of it when he gets home, so she keeps the bird. The next week, he comes back after a long sales trip.

"Look at what I bought, honey," she says to him.

The parrot looks at her husband and says, "Awwk. Whores for twenty bucks! Awwk! New whores! Awwk! Hi, Bob."

A mother is explaining sex to her young son.

"You see, Timmy, a man has a penis and a woman has a vagina. And when you put a penis in a vagina, you get a baby."

"I see," Timmy says. "But last night I saw Daddy put his penis in your mouth. What's that get?"

"Jewelry," his mom explained.

A spinster left specific instructions in her will for her tombstone inscription. It was to read: "Born a virgin, lived a virgin, died a virgin." But the stonecutters got lazy, knowing their were no survivors to complain. The spinster's tombstone reads: "Returned unopened."

Millions of sperm are racing into the darkness, fired up over their mission, when one yells to the front, "How much farther to the ovaries?"

The one in front shouts back, "Could be a while. We just passed the tonsils."

A woman takes her dog to the vet.

"He's always trying to hump me. What can I do?"

The vet looks at the Great Dane, then says, "I'd recommend castration."

The woman frowns. "That sounds awfully drastic. Couldn't you just trim his nails and do something about his breath?"

**Q:** WHAT DID THE WOMAN DO WHEN SHE HEARD THAT 90 PERCENT OF ALL CRIMES OCCUR AROUND THE HOME?

**A:** She moved.

An ad in the personals section of a local newspaper:

> A tall, well-built woman with great
> sense of humor, who can cook frog
> legs and who really likes a good fuc-
> hsia garden, classical music, and tal-
> king without getting too serious.

Please read only lines 1, 3, and 5.

**Q:** HOW DO YOU TELL WHEN YOUR WIFE IS DEAD?

**A:** The sex is the same, but the dishes pile up.

Nurses tending to a woman in a coma notice some brain activity while washing her private parts. Elated, they summon her husband with an odd announcement: "We think oral sex might actually revive her."

The husband agrees to try, and the nurses leave him alone with his wife.

Five minutes later, her heart monitor is sounding an alarm. The nurses rip back the curtain to find the man stepping off the bed and zipping up his pants.

"I didn't work," he said. "I think she choked!"

There was a group of people waiting for a bus at the station. When the bus pulled up, a line formed to get on. The first person was a lovely woman wearing a very revealing miniskirt. She tried and tried to step up onto the bus, but her skirt was too tight. She reached around behind and unzipped her zipper a bit, and tried again. No luck. So she unzipped her zipper a bit more. No matter—her skirt was still too tight. Finally, she unzipped her zipper all the way and tried to get on. Her skirt was *still* too tight. Suddenly the man behind her picked her up around the waist and carried her onto the bus. She turned around angrily.

"How dare you touch me like that?" she said vehemently.

"Well," he said, "after you unzipped my zipper all the way, I decided that we were pretty good friends."

TENTH-GRADE BOY: What's your favorite subject?

TENTH-GRADE GIRL: Poetry.

TENTH-GRADE BOY: Good. Can you help me with my Longfellow?

Q: HOW DO YOU STOP A WOMAN FROM GIVING BLOW JOBS?
A: Marry her.

One beautiful autumn afternoon, two old crones were sitting and talking in a park. Along came a flasher who flashed the two old ladies. One had a stroke. The other couldn't reach that far.

Q: WHY DO BLONDES WEAR FLANNEL PANTIES?
A: To keep their ankles warm.

Q: WHY ARE BLOND WOMEN SO EASY?
A: Who cares?

A man and his young wife were in divorce court, and the custody of their children posed a problem. The mother leaped to her feet and protested to the judge that since she brought the children into this world, she should keep custody of them. The man also wanted custody, and the judge asked him to justify his request.

After a long silence, the man slowly rose from his chair and replied, "Your Honor, when I put a dollar in a vending machine and a Coke comes out, does the Coke belong to me or to the machine?"

**Q:** HOW CAN YOU TELL MODELS ARE JUST A LITTLE SMARTER THAN COWS?

**A:** When you squeeze their tits, they don't crap on your head.

**Q:** WHY DON'T WOMEN GO SKIING?

**A:** There's no snow between the kitchen and the bathroom.

**Q:** HOW CAN YOU TELL WHEN A WOMAN REACHES ORGASM?

**A:** She drops her nail file.

**Q:** WHAT'S THE DIFFERENCE BETWEEN A LAWYER AND A HOOKER?

**A:** A hooker stops screwing you once you're dead.

**Q:** WHAT DID ONE DOE SAY TO THE OTHER DOE ON THE WAY OUT OF THE WOODS?

**A:** I'll never do that for two bucks again.

Before marriage, a man yearns for the woman he loves. After marriage, the *Y* becomes silent.

How about the woman who was so ugly, she walked into a 7-Eleven and they turned off the surveillance cameras?

Q: WHAT'S THE DIFFERENCE BETWEEN IN-LAWS AND OUT-LAWS?
A: Outlaws are wanted.

A woman was given her first matzoh ball. "This is delicious," she said. "Does the rest of the matzoh taste this good?"

Q: HOW MANY WOMEN DOES IT TAKE TO SCREW IN A LIGHTBULB?
A: One. She just holds it while the world revolves around her.

A man was confiding to his drinking buddy at a bar. "Last night was awful. I got drunk and was screwing my wife. I was so bombed that when we were finished, I handed her a twenty-dollar bill."

"Oh," the friend said, "that *is* bad."

"It gets worse. She handed me back ten dollars in change."

A young model is engaged to a ninety-seven-year-old oil tycoon. She is talking to the caterer about the wedding reception and insisting that the festivities having a football theme.

"Football," the caterer asks. "Why?"

"Well," the young woman replies, "I am hoping he's going to kick off soon."

Two boys are talking.

"My daddy has a penis."

"My daddy has two."

"Huh?"

"A little one he pees with, and a big one he uses to clean the baby-sitter's teeth."

On their wedding night, a man tells his new wife, "There will always be a box under our bed, but you must promise to never look inside it."

She agrees, but after forty years, curiosity gets to her. She opens the box only to find three empty beer bottles and $3,000 in one-dollar bills.

Five years later, she can't stand it anymore and wakes her husband in the middle of the night to ask about what she found.

"Well," the husband explains, "every time I was unfaithful to you, I chugged a bottle of beer and put the empty in the box."

"I see," the wife says. "I guess three women in forty years isn't so bad."

They go back to sleep, but a while later the woman wakes him up again.

"Wait a minute," she says. "What about the $3,000? What's that?"

"I had to put the money from all the bottles I returned *somewhere*!"

Blonde Invention Number 279: solar-powered flashlights.

A man comes home to tell his wife a horrible story about being on the golf course that day. "Sam brought along his mother to play with Frank and me because Stan couldn't make it. And the lady dropped dead on the fourth green!"

"Oh, honey! How awful!"

"It really was. Fourteen holes of, 'Hit the ball! Drag Mother! Hit the ball! Drag Mother!' "

Two men were riding a motorcycle on a cold, blustery day. When it became too windy for the passenger, he put his jacket on backward to keep the wind from blowing it open. A few miles down the road, the motorcycle hit a tree, killing the driver instantly and stunning the passenger.

Later, when a detective visited the scene, he asked a cop standing nearby what happened.

"Well," the officer replied, "one of them was dead when I got here, and by the time I got the other one's head straightened around, he was dead, too."

**Q:** WHY DO THEY CALL IT PMS?
**A:** Because Mad Cow Disease was already taken.

**Q:** WHAT HAPPENED TO THE BLONDE WHO LOCKED HER KEYS IN HER CAR?
**A:** It took her three hours to get her family out.

Have you heard about the woman who studied for a blood test, and failed it?

The teacher questioned one of her students, a young blonde.

"Susie," she said. "Can you explain to me why this essay is in your boyfriend's handwriting?"

"Sure," Susie replied. "I used his pen."

An older farmer finds he is too tired for sex in the evening, or even the afternoon. He has erections only occasionally, usually in the middle of the day while he is out in the field. To keep his wife satisfied, he brings a shotgun with him on the tractor. Each time she hears the gun fire into the air, she runs out to the field to make love.

"It worked great all summer," the farmer told his neighbor. "Then hunting season started, and I haven't seen her since."

Two women were driving through the middle of Kansas, where there was nothing around for miles but wheat fields. One says, "Look over there!" There was a woman wearing scuba gear trying to swim through the wheat.

The other says, "Look over *there*," pointing at still another woman in a boat, rowing through the wheat.

The woman driving says, "It's women like that that give us a bad name."

The second woman says, "Yeah! And if I knew how to swim, I'd go out there and beat the crap out of them!"

On the way back from a dinner celebrating their fifteenth wedding anniversary, a couple is involved in a gruesome accident. The husband survives with only a broken arm, but the wife's face is horribly disfigured. A plastic surgeon said a skin graft is the only remedy, but the woman is too thin to offer much spare flesh. It will have to come from her husband's buttocks.

They agree to the procedure, and to keep it a secret— particularly the source of the grafted flesh.

At home months later, the wife turns to her husband with her gorgeous new face and says, "Oh, honey, you've given me so much. How can I ever repay you?"

"You don't have to," he replies. "I get thanks enough every time I see your mother kiss you on the cheek."

A blond bank robber runs out through the front door of a bank lugging a heavy metal safe with rope tied all around it. A security guard with his pants around his ankles chases after her.

"You idiot!" the getaway driver yells at her. "I told you to tie up the GUARD and blow the SAFE!"

Element Name: WOMAN

Symbol: WO

Atomic Weight: (don't even go there!)

Physical properties: Boils at nothing and may freeze anytime. Melts whenever treated properly. Very bitter if not used well.

Chemical properties: Active, often unstable. Possesses strong molecular attraction to gold, silver, platinum, and precious stones.

Usage: An extremely good catalyst for dispersion of wealth. Probably the most powerful income-reducing agent known.

Caution: Highly explosive in inexperienced hands.

A beautiful blonde flops down in First Class on a flight from Los Angeles bound for New York. A flight attendant approaches her to say her ticket is only good for Coach.

"But I am beautiful, I am a blonde, and I am heading for New York City," she replies. "I deserve First Class."

Frustrated, the flight attendant summons her boss, who also asks the blonde to move back into Coach.

"Don't you see how beautiful I am," the blonde replies. "I'm a blonde and blondes fly First Class."

Finally, the pilot walks back to speak to her. After a few moments, the blonde hops up and takes a seat in the back, near the rest room.

"What did you tell her?" the flight attendant asks.

"I told her First Class wasn't going to New York," says the pilot.

A woman announces to her friend that she is getting married for the fourth time.

"How wonderful! But I hope you don't mind my asking what happened to your first husband?"

"He ate poisonous fish and died."

"Oh, how tragic! What about your second husband?"

"He ate poisonous fish, too, and died."

"Oh, how terrible! I'm almost afraid to ask you about your third husband."

"He died of a broken neck."

"How did that happen?"

"He wouldn't eat the fish."

A husband and wife are out playing golf. They tee off and one drive goes to the right and one drive goes to the left. The wife finds her ball in a patch of buttercups. Terrible at the game, she begins hacking through the flowers trying to advance the ball. Suddenly there's a cloud of smoke, and a woman wearing leaves and flowers and flowing robes appears and announces, "I'm Mother Nature, and I don't like the way you treated my buttercups. From now on, you won't be able to stand the taste of butter. Each time you eat butter you will become physically ill to the point of total nausea."

The mystery woman then disappears as quickly as she appeared. Shaken, the wife calls out to her husband, "Hey, where are you?"

"Over here," he yells back. "My ball landed in a bunch of pussy willows."

"Don't hit it!" the wife screams. "For God's sake, don't hit it!"

A scientist, an astrologer, and a blonde escape a burning building by climbing to the roof. The firemen are on the street below, holding a blanket for them to jump into.

The firemen yell to the scientist, "Jump! Jump! It's your only chance to survive!"

The scientist jumps and—*swish!*—the firemen yank the blanket away. The scientist slams into the sidewalk like a rock.

"C'mon! Jump! You gotta jump!" say the firemen to the astrologer.

"Oh no! You'll pull the blanket away!" cries the astrologer.

"No! It's scientists we can't stand! We *like* astrologers!" they call back.

"Okay," says the astrologer, and she jumps. *Swish!* The firemen yank the blanket away, and the lady is flattened on the pavement.

Finally, the blonde steps to the edge of the roof.

Again, the firemen yell, "Jump! You have to jump!"

"No way!" the blonde yells back. "You're just gonna pull the blanket away!"

"No! Really! You have to jump! We won't pull the blanket away!" say the firemen.

"Look," the blonde says, "Nothing you say is gonna convince me that you're not gonna pull the blanket away! So what I want you to do is put the blanket down and back away from it . . ."

A sales executive was helping a new blond trainee prepare for her first weekend sales convention. Upon their arrival in Dallas, the boss showed her the best places to eat, shop, and stay overnight. The next morning, as the executive was organizing sales materials for the day's presentation, he noticed the trainee was missing. He called up to her room to ask what happened to her. She answered the phone, crying, and said, "I can't get out of my room!"

"You can't get out of your room?" the executive asked. "Why not?"

"There are only three doors in here," she sobbed. "One is the bathroom, one is the closet, and one has a sign on it that says DO NOT DISTURB!"

A blonde, a scientist, and an astronomer were trying out for a new NASA experiment on sending women to different planets. First, they called the scientist in and asked her a question.

"If you could go to any planet, what planet would you want to go to and why?"

After pondering the question, she answered, "I would like to go to Mars because it seems the most likely planet in the solar system to have life, in addition to Earth."

They thanked her and said they would get back to her. Next, the astronomer entered the room and the NASA people asked her the same question.

"I would like to go to Saturn to see all of its rings," she said.

"Thank you," they said, and they told her they would get back to her.

Finally, the blonde entered the room and they asked her the same question they asked the other two.

She thought for a while and then replied, "I would like to go to the sun."

Surprised by her answer, the people from NASA said, "Don't you know that if you went to the sun, you would burn to death?"

"Do you think I'm stupid?" she replied. "I'd go at night!"

**Q:** HOW MANY WOMAN JOKES ARE THERE?
**A:** Just this one. The rest are all true stories.

An eighteen-year-old girl from a strict family finally had the opportunity to go to a party by herself. Since she was very good-looking, she was a bit nervous about what to do if boys approached her. Her mom said, "It's very easy! Whenever a boy starts hitting on you, you ask him, 'What will be the name of our baby?' That'll scare him off."

So off she went. After a little while at the party, a boy started dancing with her, and little by little he started kissing her and touching her.

She said to him, "What will our baby be called?"

The boy found some excuse and disappeared. Sometime later, the same thing happened again: A boy danced with her, and then started to kiss her neck and shoulders. She stopped him and asked about the baby's name, and off he ran, just like the first.

Later on, another boy invited her for a walk. After a few minutes, he started kissing her, and she asked him, "What will our baby be called?"

He continued, now slowly taking her clothes off.

"What will our baby be called?" she asked once more. Meanwhile, he removed all her clothes and began to have sex with her.

"What will our baby be called?" she asked him again.

When he was done, he took off his condom, tied a knot in it, and said, "If he gets out of this one, I'll call him Houdini!"

A blonde is terribly overweight, so her doctor puts her on a diet.

"I want you to eat regularly for a day, then skip a

day, and then repeat this procedure for two weeks. The next time I see you, you'll have lost at least five pounds."

When the blonde returns to see the doctor, she's lost nearly twenty pounds.

"Why, that's amazing!" the doctor says. "Did you follow my instructions?"

The blonde nods. "I'll tell you, though, I thought I was going to drop dead that second day," she says.

"From hunger, you mean?" he says.

"No, from skipping."

How about the woman who walked into the lobby of a building and a saw a sign saying, WET FLOOR. So she did.

A woman was filling out an application for a job. She promptly filled in the spaces calling for *name, age, address* and so forth. Then she came to the space saying *salary expected.*

"Yes," she wrote in.

Bill pilled up a stool in his favorite bar and announced, "My wife, Kate, must love me more than any woman has ever loved any man!"

"What makes you say that?" the bartender inquired.

"Last week," Bill explained, "I had to take a couple of

sick days from work. Kate was so happy to have me around that every time the milkman and the mailman came by, she'd run down the driveway, waving her arms and hollering, 'My old man's home! My old man's home!'"

Three women—a blonde, a brunette, and a redhead—who work in the same office notice that their boss, also a woman, has started leaving work early every day. One day they decide that after she leaves, they'll take off early, too. After all, how is she to know?

The brunette is thrilled to get home early. She does a little needlework, watches a movie, and then goes to bed.

The redhead is elated to be able to get in a quick workout at her gym before meeting a dinner date.

The blonde is also very happy to be home early, but on her way upstairs she hears noises coming from her bedroom. She quietly opens the door a crack and is mortified to see her husband in bed with her boss! Ever so gently, she closes the door and creeps down the stairs and out of the house.

The next day, the brunette and the redhead talk about leaving early again, but when they ask the blonde if she wants to leave, too, she shakes her head.

"No way!" she says. "Yesterday I almost got caught!"

Two models are shopping at the mall. When they are done they go out to their car, which happens to be a convertible with a leather interior. When they reach the car, they realize they had locked the keys in the ignition. So they both kind of stand there and think for a while. Then one has the idea to try to open the car with a hanger. So the first model starts using a hanger to fiddle with the lock. The other model looks up at the sky and suddenly becomes very worried.

"Hurry," she urges. "It's going to rain and we left the top down!"

A few guys always get together after work for a drink at the local watering hole. One Friday, Jeb showed up late, sat down at the bar, and powered down his entire first beer in one huge gulp. Then he turned to Bob and said, "Times are getting tough, my friend. Today my wife told me that she's going to cut back sex with me to just twice a week. I can't believe it."

Bob put his hand on Jeb's shoulder and said reassuringly, "You think you've got it bad? She's cut some guys out all together!"

A blonde walks into a pharmacy and asks for anal deodorant.

"Ma'am," the clerk says, "such a thing does not exist."

"Sure it does," she replies. "I got a stick a few weeks ago that said 'Push Up from Bottom.' "

**Q:** WHAT DID THE WOMAN SAY WHEN SHE SAW A BOX OF CHEERIOS?

**A:** "Neat . . . doughnut seeds!"

A man wanted to find out if both his wife and mistress were faithful to him. So he decided to send them on the same cruise, then later question each one about the other's behavior. When his wife returned, he asked her about the people on the trip in general, then casually asked her about the specific behavior of the passenger he knew to be his mistress.

"She was a real tramp. She slept with nearly every man on the ship," his wife reported.

The disheartened man then rendezvoused with his cheating mistress to ask her the same questions about his wife. "She was a real lady," his mistress said.

"How so?" the man asked.

"She came on board with her husband and never left his side."

A well-built, young blonde was on her psychiatrist's couch, telling him how frustrated she was with her attempts to launch a career.

"I tried to be an actress and failed," she complained. "I tried to be an executive assistant and failed. I tried being a writer and failed. I tried being a salesclerk and I failed at that, too."

The shrink thought for a moment and said, "Everyone needs to live a full, satisfying life. Why don't you try nursing?"

The girl thinks about this, then bares one of her beautiful breasts, points it at the shrink, and says, "If you're willing, go ahead."

A woman is walking down the street with a pig under her arm. She passes a person who asks, "Where did you get that?"

The pig says, "I won her in a raffle!"

A man comes home from a night of drinking. As he falls through the doorway of his house, his wife snaps at him, "What's the big idea coming home half drunk?"

The man replies, "I'm sorry, honey. I ran out of money."

A blonde, a redhead, and a brunette board a double-decker bus to go sightseeing in London. There are two seats left on the bottom of the bus and one seat on the top when they board. They decide to take turns riding on the top and flip a coin to see who gets the first turn. The blonde wins the toss.

A couple of hours later, it's the redhead's turn. When she walks up the stairs, she sees the blonde sitting there quaking, scared to death.

"What's wrong?" the redhead asks. "This is a great way to see the city."

"Sure, but at least you've got a driver down there," the blonde replies.

Q: WHY DO WOMEN LIKE CARS WITH ADJUSTABLE STEER-ING WHEELS?
A: More headroom.

A man was wandering around a fairground and he happened to see a fortune-teller's booth. Thinking it would be good for a laugh, he went inside and sat down.

"Ah . . ." said the woman as she gazed into her crystal ball. "I see you are the father of three children."

"Close," the man said, chuckling. "I'm actually the father of four children."

The woman smiled and said, "That's what *you* think!"

Q: WHY DID THE BLONDE DECIDE TO DATE HUNTERS?
A: Because she heard they go deep into the bush, always shoot twice, love to mount their prey, and always eat what they shoot.

Q: HOW MANY MEN DOES IT TAKE TO OPEN A BEER?
A: None. It should be open by the time she takes it to him.

One day, a man walks into a dentist's office and asks how much it will cost to extract wisdom teeth.

"Ninety dollars," the dentist says.

"That's ridiculous," the man says. "Can't it be done any cheaper?"

"Well," the dentist says. "If you don't use an anesthetic, I can knock the price down to sixty dollars."

Looking annoyed, the man says, "That's still too expensive!"

"Okay," says the dentist. "If I save on anesthesia and simply rip the teeth out with a pair of pliers, I can knock the price down to twenty dollars."

"Nope," moans the man, "it's still too much."

"Well," says the dentist, scratching his head, "if I let one of my students do it, I suppose I can knock the price down to ten dollars."

"Marvelous," says the man. "Book my wife for next Tuesday!"

**Q:** DID YOU HEAR ABOUT THE NEW BLONDE PAINT?
**A:** It's not real bright, but it's cheap, and spreads easy.

**Q:** WHY CAN'T A BLONDE COUNT PAST SIXTY-EIGHT?
**A:** Because sixty-nine is a mouthful.

**Q:** WHY DO NURSES MAKE BAD LOVERS?

**A:** They always wait for the swelling to go down.

**Q:** WHAT DO SMART MODELS AND UFOS HAVE IN COMMON?

**A:** You always hear about them but never see them.

A blonde goes to the doctor complaining that both of her ears are burned.

"How did this happen?" asks the doctor.

"Well, I was ironing and the phone rang. By mistake, I picked up the iron instead of the phone."

"But what happened to the other ear?" says the doctor.

"The idiot called back," she replies.

An older couple has suffered with sexual boredom for years. To spice things up, the wife buys some crotchless panties from a catalog. That night, in the bedroom, she removes her nightgown to reveal her new underwear.

"You want some?" she asks her husband in a breathy voice.

"Lord, no!" he yells. "Look what it did to your panties!"

Cindy was seen going into the woods with a small package and a birdcage. She was gone several days and then finally returned. Her friend Linda had never seen Cindy looking so sad.

"I heard you went off in the woods for a couple of days," Linda said. "I'm glad you got back okay, but why do you look so sad?"

Cindy replied, "Because I just can't get a man."

Linda said, "Well, you sure won't find one in the middle of the woods."

"Don't be so silly," Cindy said. "I know that. I went into the woods because I needed something there that would get me a man. But I just couldn't find it."

"I don't understand," Linda said. "What are you talking about?"

"I went there to catch a couple of owls," Cindy replied. "I took some dead mice and a birdcage."

"How on earth will that help you get a man?" asked Linda.

"Well," said Cindy, "I'm told the best way to get a man is to have a good pair of hooters."

Q: WHAT DO YOU DO IF A MODEL THROWS A GRENADE AT YOU?
A: Pull the pin and throw it back.

Three blondes are stuck on a desert island, and one day one of them finds a magic lamp.

They rub it and a genie pops out and gives them each a wish.

The first one says, "I wish I was 10 percent smarter so I could get off of this island."

Then she turns into a redhead and swims off the island.

The second sees what happens and says, "I wish I was 25 percent smarter so that I could get off this island!"

She then turns into a brunette, makes a raft from some trees, and sails away.

Finally, the third blonde says, "I wish I was 50 percent smarter so that I could get off this island."

She then suddenly turns into a man and walks across the bridge.

A sixth-grade biology teacher, Mrs. Hart, says to her class, "Who can tell me which organ of the human body expands to ten times its usual size when stimulated?"

Nobody raises a hand, so she calls on the first student to look her way.

"Mary, can you tell me which organ of the human body expands to ten times its usual size when stimulated?"

Mary blushes. "Mrs. Hart, how dare you ask such a question?" she says. "I'm going to complain to my parents, who will complain to the principal, who will have you fired!"

Mrs. Hart is surprised by Mary's reaction but undaunted. She asks the class the question again, and this time Sam raises his hand.

"Yes, Sam?" she says.

"Mrs. Hart, the correct answer is the iris of the human eye."

"Very good, Sam," says the teacher. "Thank you."

Mrs. Hart then turns to Mary and says, "Mary, I have three things to tell you. First, it's clear that you have *not* done your homework. Second, you have a *dirty* mind. And third, one day you are going to be sadly disappointed."

A guy who's been drinking heavily in a bar staggers over a woman sitting nearby. With no warning, he puts his hand up her skirt, so she slaps him.

"Oh, I'm sorry," he says. "You look like my wife."

"What a worthless, fucking asshole you are!" she says scornfully.

"Wow," he says. "You sound like her, too!"

How to impress a woman:

Compliment her

cuddle her

kiss her

caress her

love her

stroke her

tease her

comfort her

protect her

hug her

hold her

spend money on her

wine and dine her

listen to her

care for her

stand by her

support her

marry her

go to the ends of the earth for her

How to impress a man:

Show up naked

bring beer

A highway patrolman pulled up alongside a speeding car on the turnpike. As the officer peered through the driver's window, he was astounded to find that the model behind the wheel was knitting. The trooper cranked down his window and yelled to the driver, "Pull over!" at the top of his lungs.

"No!" the model yelled back. "Hat!"

A married man decided to stay at work late to be with his sexy new marketing assistant, so he called his wife to make up an excuse. After work, he invited the assistant to dinner. After dinner, the two went back to her apartment and had great sex for two hours. When he went to the bathroom to straighten up for the trip home, he noticed a huge hickey on his neck. The whole way home, he went nuts wondering what he was going to tell his wife.

After the man unlocked the front door, his dog came bounding to greet him. "That's it!" the man thought, and promptly fell to the carpet, pretending to fight off the affectionate canine.

Holding his neck with one hand, he went upstairs and said, "Honey, look what the dog did to my neck!"

"Hell, that's nothing," she answered, opening her blouse. "Look what he did to my tits!"

Q: WHAT DO SOME WOMEN PUT BEHIND THEIR EARS BEFORE SEX?
A: Their ankles.

Four women go out in one of their boyfriends' pickup trucks. Three of the women sit in the cab up front, and the fourth sits in the open truck bed in the back. The three go inside a honky-tonk, but the fourth doesn't join them for an hour.

"What took you so long?" one asked her.

"No one told me how to get the tailgate open."

**Q:** WHAT DOES A SCREEN DOOR HAVE IN COMMON WITH A MODEL?

**A:** The more you bang it, the looser it gets!

**Q:** WHAT'S THE DIFFERENCE BETWEEN A WOMAN WITH PMS AND AN ENRAGED COW?

**A:** Lipstick.

**Q:** WHAT DO YOU CALL A BASEMENT FULL OF GIRL-FRIENDS?

**A:** A whine cellar.

There was a blonde and a redhead in an elevator. On their way down, the elevator stops to pick up a man. When he gets on, the girls notice that although he is pretty cute, unfortunately he has dandruff. On their way off of the elevator, the two girls let the man go ahead of them.

The redhead turns to the blonde and says, "Oh, my God! We should give him Head & Shoulders."

The blonde replies, "That's what I was thinking. Except how do you give a guy Shoulders?"

Q: WHAT'S THE DIFFERENCE BETWEEN YOUR NEW WIFE
   AND YOUR JOB?
A: After five years, your job will still suck.

Q: WHAT DID THE BLONDE SELL FOR GAS MONEY?
A: Her car.

There were these three women who escaped from prison, a
blonde and two redheads. To get away from the cops they
hide in an abandoned farmhouse. In the farmhouse there
are three burlap sacks, so they hide in them. When the cops
come to the farmhouse, one of them sees the sacks.

"There's just three burlap sacks in here!" he yells.

His partner replies, "Kick them just to be sure no one's
hiding in them."

The first officer kicks a sack with one of the redheads
in it and she yells, "MEEEYYOWW!"

The officer says, "Oh, it's just a stupid cat in there."

So he kicks the one with the other redhead in it and she
yells, "RUFFF! RUFFF!"

The officer says, "Oh, it's just a stupid dog."

Then he kicks the sack with the blonde in it and she
yells, "POTATOES!"

Q: WHY ARE MEN SMARTER THAN WOMEN?
A: Two heads are better than one.

**Q:** WHAT DID THE BLONDE WRITE IN THE BOX THAT SAID *SIGN HERE* ON HER EMPLOYMENT APPLICATION?
**A:** Capricorn.

A blonde goes to see her doctor and says, "Doc, I hurt all over."

Confused, the doctor says, "What do you mean, you hurt all over?"

The blonde says, "I'll show you."

She then touches herself on her leg. "OW!!! I hurt there."

Then she touches her earlobe. "OW!!!!!! I hurt there, too!"

Then she touches her hair. "OW!!!!! Even my hair hurts!"

So the doctor sits back and thinks for a minute or two. Then he says, "Tell me, is blond your natural hair color?"

The model says, "Yes, why?"

"I thought so," the doctor replies. "You have a broken finger."

After extensive testing, scientists have discovered that beer contains female hormones. The study involved 500 men who consumed large quantities of beer in a single sitting.

The researchers found that 100 percent of the men:

81

1. Gained weight.

2. Talked excessively without making sense.

3. Became emotional.

4. Called home just to see if anyone called.

5. Couldn't drive.

6. Went to the bathroom in groups.

**Q:** WHERE DID THE BLONDE ASK HER DATE TO MEET HER?
**A:** At the corner of Walk and Don't Walk.

A blonde and a redhead were watching the six-o'clock news together. There was a news story about a man poised to jump off a bridge. The redhead turned to the blonde and said, "I bet you twenty dollars he jumps."

The blonde replied, "You're on."

Sure enough, the man jumped, and the blonde gave the redhead twenty dollars.

Feeling bad, the redhead said, "I can't accept the money. I watched the five-o'clock news and saw the man jump then."

"No, you can take it," said the blonde. "I watched the five-o'clock news, too, but I didn't think he would jump again."

**Q:** A BLONDE, A BRUNETTE, AND A REDHEAD ARE ALL IN NINTH GRADE TOGETHER. WHO HAS THE BIGGEST TITS?

**A:** The blonde. She's nineteen.

As a blonde crawled out of her wrecked car, the cop on the scene asked her what happened.

The blonde began, "It was the scariest thing! I looked up and saw a tree, so I swerved to the right. Then I saw another tree, so I swerved to left. Then there was another tree, and another and another . . ."

The cop thought for a minute and then said, "Ma'am, there are only cornfields for the next twenty miles. But you might want to take your air freshener down the next time you drive."

A young ventriloquist is touring the clubs and stops to entertain at a bar in a small town. He's going through his usual run of stupid-blonde jokes, when a large, blond woman in the fourth row stands on her chair and says, "I've heard just about enough of your denigrating jokes! What makes you think you can stereotype women that way? What does a woman's physical attributes have to do with her value as a human being?"

The ventriloquist is stunned.

"It's guys like you who keep women like me from being respected at work and in my community," she continues. "And of reaching my full potential as a person because you and your kind continue to perpetuate discrimination against all women—all in the name of humor."

Flustered, the ventriloquist begins to apologize. The woman interjects, "You stay out of this, mister. I'm talking to that little bastard on your knee!"

A drunk is driving through town and his car is weaving from one side of the road to the other. A cop pulls him over.

"So," says the cop, "where have you been?"

"I've been to a bar," slurs the drunk.

"Well," says the cop, "it looks like you've had quite a few. "

"I might have," the drunk says.

"Did you know," says the cop, "that a few intersections back, your wife fell out of your car?"

"Oh, thank the Lord," replies the drunk. "For a couple of minutes, I thought I'd gone deaf."

A man was in his front yard mowing grass when an attractive blond neighbor came out of her house and walked straight to her mailbox. She opened it, then slammed it shut and stomped back to her house. A little later, she came out, went to the mailbox, opened it, and slammed it shut again. She again stomped back to her house. When the man was almost finished with his lawn, she came out once more. She walked purposefully to the mailbox, opened it, and then slammed it shut harder than before.

By now curious, the man asked, "Is something wrong?"

"There certainly is!" the woman replied. "My stupid

computer keeps sending me a message saying 'You've Got Mail.' "

A woman goes to a bar and sits drinking shots of whiskey all evening. She eventually passes out and all the men have their way with her. She comes in the next Friday night and does the same thing. And the next Friday, and the next after that.

One Friday she walks in and says to the bartender, "Give me a shot of tequila."

"I thought you drink whiskey?"

"Not anymore," she says. "It makes my pussy sore."

A blonde went to a flight school insisting she wanted to learn to fly. As all the planes were currently in use, the instructor agreed to teach her by radio how to pilot the solo helicopter.

He took her out, showed her how to start it, and gave her the basics. Then he sent her on her way. After she climbed 1,000 feet, she radioed in.

"I'm doing great! I love it! The view is beautiful, and I'm really starting to get the hang of this."

After 3,000 feet, she radioed again, saying how easy it was to fly. The instructor watched her climb over 3,000 feet, and then began to worry when she didn't radio in again. A few minutes later, he watched in horror as she crashed about a half mile away. He ran to the site as fast as he could and pulled her from the wreckage.

When he asked what happened, she said, "I don't know.

Everything was going fine, but as I got higher, I started to get cold. And I can't remember anything after I turned off the big fan!"

Trapped on an elevator with six people for two days, a woman finally stands up and announces, "If I'm going to die, I want to die feeling like a woman."

She removes every stitch of her clothing and asks, "Is there someone on this elevator who is man enough to make me feel like a woman?"

A man stands up, rips off his shirt, and marches over to the woman.

"Here," he says. "Iron this."

A man was approached by a coworker who invited him out for a few beers after work. The man said that his wife would hate it, that she didn't allow him to go out drinking with the boys after work.

"Come out with us," suggested the coworker. "When you get home tonight, sneak into the house, gently climb in under the sheets, pull down your wife's panties, and give her oral sex. She'll love it, and she'll never mention that you went out drinking."

The man agreed to try it, and went out and enjoyed himself. Late that night, he sneaked into the house and saw his wife asleep on the couch. He left the lights off and gently slid down his wife's panties and gave her oral sex. She moaned and groaned with pleasure, but after a little while, he realized he had to take a leak, so he went upstairs to the bathroom. When he opened the door and went in, he was stunned to see his wife sitting on the commode.

"What are you doing in here?" he asked.

"Shhhhh!" she hushed him. "Don't wake up my mother!"

Q: HOW DO YOU KNOW A BLONDE HAS BEEN IN THE REFRIGERATOR?
A: There is lipstick on the carrot.

Q: HOW ARE WOMEN AND TORNADOES ALIKE?
A: They both moan like hell when they come, and take the house when they leave.

A guy met a girl in a bar and asks, "May I buy you a drink?"

"Okay," she says. "But it won't do you any good."

A little later, he asks, "May I buy you another drink?"

"Okay," she says again. "But it won't do you any good."

He invites her up to his apartment and she replies, "Okay, but I'm telling you, it won't do you any good."

They get to his apartment and he says, "You are the most beautiful woman I've ever seen. I want you for my wife."

"Oh, well, that's different," she says. "Send her in!"

A grocery clerk sweeping up the juices aisle notices a blonde staring intently at an orange-juice container.

"Can I help you, miss?" he asks.

"Shhhh!" she says. "It says 'concentrate.'"

A guy walks into a sperm bank wearing a ski mask and carrying a gun. He goes up to the nurse and demands that she open the vault.

"But, sir, this a sperm bank!" she says.

"I don't care, open it now!" he says.

So she opens the door to the vault and inside are all the sperm samples.

The robber says, "Take one of those sperm samples and drink it!"

"But they're sperm samples!" she replies, shocked.

"Just do it," he growls.

So she sucks it back.

Then the man removes his mask and tells the woman, "See, honey, it's just not that difficult."

Two drunks are sitting at a bar, staring into their drinks.

One gets a funny look on his face and asks, "Hey, Bill, have you ever seen an ice cube with a hole in it before?"

"Sure," says Bill. "I've been married to one for twenty-five years!"

Q: WHAT DO YOU CALL A DEAD BLONDE IN A CLOSET?

**A:** Last year's hide-and-go-seek champion.

A gorgeous woman walks into a doctor's office. The doctor is bowled over by how stunningly beautiful she is. As he begins to examine her, all his professionalism goes right out the window.

He tells her to take off her slacks, and he starts rubbing her inner thighs.

"Do you know what I am doing?" asks the doctor.

"Yes, checking for abnormalities," she replies.

He tells her to take off her shirt and bra, which she does. The doctor begins rubbing her breasts and asks, "Do you know what I am doing now?"

"Yes, checking for cancer," she replies.

Finally, he tells her to take off her panties and puts her on the examining table. He gets on top of her and starts having sex with her.

He says, "Do you know what I am doing now?"

"Of course," she replies. "You're getting herpes. That's what I'm here to be treated for."

**Q:** WHY DON'T BLONDES WATER-SKI?
**A:** Because they lie down as soon as their crotches get wet.

**Q:** WHAT DO YOU CALL A GROUP OF BLONDES ON ROLLER SKATES?

**A:** A mobile sperm bank.

One day Mr. Jones, the president of a large corporation, called one of his vice presidents, Mr. Herbert, into his office.

"We have to make some cutbacks in your department, so either Jack or Denise will have to be laid off," he said.

Mr. Herbert said, "Denise is my best worker, but Jack has a wife and three kids. I'm not sure which one to fire."

"You decide," replied Mr. Jones.

The next morning Mr. Herbert waited for his employees to arrive. Denise was the first to come in, so he said to her, "Denise, I've got a problem. You see, I've got to lay you or Jack off and I don't know which to do."

Denise replied, "You'd better jack off. I've got a headache this morning."

A man is preparing for a date with a hot model and decides to get tan all over. Unfortunately, he falls asleep in the sun and his cock gets badly sunburned. He rubs lotion all over it, but by the time he gets to her house for dinner, it's starting to sting again.

After dinner, his date pours them both a glass of milk for the dessert cake. Then she excuses herself to freshen up. He takes the opportunity to douse his cock in the milk to cool it down.

She walks back into the room and freezes at the sight of what's happening.

"So that's how you guys reload those things!" she finally says.

The Queen of England was visiting one of London's top hospitals, and during her tour of the floors, she passed a room where a male patient was masturbating.

"Oh, my God!" said the Queen. "What is the meaning of this!"

The doctor leading the tour explained, "I'm sorry, Your Highness, this man has a very serious condition in which the testicles rapidly fill with semen. If he doesn't do that five times a day, they will explode and he would surely die instantly."

"Oh, I am sorry," said the Queen.

On the next floor they passed a room where a young nurse was giving a patient a blow job.

"Oh, my God!" said the Queen. "Whatever is happening in there!"

The doctor replied, "Same problem, better health plan."

Q: HOW IS A BLONDE DIFFERENT FROM FIRST CLASS?
A: Some guys have never been in First Class.

Q: WHAT DO YOU GET WHEN YOU OFFER A BLONDE A PENNY FOR HER THOUGHTS?
A: Change.

Three sisters wanted to get married, but their parents couldn't afford three weddings, so they held all three together on the same day. They also couldn't afford to go on honeymoons, so they all stayed home with their new husbands. That night, their mother got up because she couldn't sleep.

When she went past her eldest daughter's room she heard screaming. Then she went to her second daughter's room and heard laughing. At her third daughter's door she heard nothing.

The next morning, after the new husbands left for work, the mother asked her eldest daughter, "Why were you screaming last night?"

The daughter replied, "Mom, you always told me if something hurt I should scream."

"That's true," she said.

She looked at her second daughter and said, "Why were you laughing so much last night?"

The daughter replied, "Mom, you always said that if something tickled I should laugh."

"That's also true," said the girls' mother.

Then the mother looked at her youngest daughter and said, "Why was it so quiet in your room last night?"

The youngest daughter replied, "Mom, you always told me I should never talk with my mouth full."

**Q:** WHAT'S THE DIFFERENCE BETWEEN A BLONDE AND A PORSCHE?

**A:** You don't lend your Porsche out to your friends.

**Q:** OF WHAT DO BLONDE BRAIN CELLS DIE?
**A:** Loneliness.

A depressed young woman was so desperate that she decided to end her life by throwing herself into the ocean. When she went down to the docks, a handsome young sailor noticed her tears and took pity on her.

"Look, you've got a lot to live for," he said to her. "I'm off to Europe in the morning, and if you like, you can stow away on my ship. I'll take good care of you and bring you food every day." Moving closer, he slipped his arm around her shoulders and added, "I'll keep you happy, and you'll keep me happy."

The girl nodded yes. After all, what did she have to lose? That night, the sailor sneaked her aboard and hid her in a lifeboat. From then on, every night he brought her three sandwiches and a piece of fruit, and they made passionate love until dawn.

Three weeks later, during a routine search, she was discovered by the captain.

"What are you doing here?" the captain asked.

She got up out of the lifeboat and said, "I have an arrangement with one of the sailors. He's taking me to Europe, and he's screwing me."

"He sure is, lady," said the captain. "This is the Staten Island Ferry."

Two blondes decide to go duck hunting. Neither one of them has ever been duck hunting before, and after several hours they still haven't bagged any.

One of the blondes looks at the other and says, "I just don't understand. Why aren't we getting any ducks?"

"I keep telling you," her friend says. "I just don't think we're throwing the dog high enough."

A blonde went down to an employment agency looking for a job.

The hiring agent said, "I have the perfect job for you. It's painting the lines down the middle of the road."

Reluctantly, the blonde took the position. She took her paint pail and began painting the lines. The first day, she painted five miles of roadway and did the job very well. The next day, however, she only painted three miles. On her third day, she painted just one mile of roadway. Concerned, her boss asked her on the fourth day why her work was slowing down so badly.

"I'm sorry, sir," she replied. "But every day the paint pail keeps getting farther and farther away."

A woman posts an ad in the newspaper: "Looking for man who won't beat me up, run away, and is great in the sack."

She gets several responses, but not one man who meets all the criteria. One day her doorbell rings. She goes to the door, and there's a man waiting.

"Hi, I'm Bob," he says. "I have no arms, so I won't beat you up, and no legs, so I won't run away."

"How do I know you're good in bed?" she asks him.

"I rang the doorbell, didn't I?" he replies.

**Q:** WHAT'S THE DIFFERENCE BETWEEN THE PANAMA
CANAL AND A BLONDE?

**A:** One is a busy ditch.

**Q:** WHAT'S THE DIFFERENCE BETWEEN AN INTELLIGENT
BLONDE AND BIGFOOT?

**A:** Bigfoot has been seen.

One Christmas Eve, Santa Claus came down the chimney
and was startled by a beautiful nineteen-year-old model.

She said, "Santa, will you stay with me?"

Santa replied, "Ho Ho Ho, gotta go, gotta go, gotta deliver these toys to good girls and boys."

So she took off her nightgown and stood there wearing
only a bra and panties.

She said, "Santa, now will you stay with me?"

Again, Santa replied, "Ho Ho Ho, gotta go, gotta go,
gotta deliver these toys to good girls and boys."

She took off everything and said, "Santa, now will you
stay with me?"

Santa replied, "Hey, Hey, Hey, gotta stay, gotta stay.
Can't get up the chimney with my pecker this way!"

A man comes home from a tough day of work looking to unwind. After a relaxing dinner with his wife, they retire to bed. Both go to their separate beds, but the man can't get to sleep.

He calls over to his wife, "My little honey-bunny, I'm lonely."

So the woman gets out of bed and crosses the room to her husband. On the way, she trips on the carpet and falls on her face.

Concerned, the husband says, "Oh, did my little baby-waby fall on her little nosey-wosey?"

The woman gets up and gets into the man's bed. The two have passionate sex, and afterward the woman rolls out. As she returns to her bed, she once again catches her foot on the carpet and falls flat on her face.

The man looks over at his wife lying on the floor and says, "Clumsy bitch!"

Q: WHAT DO YOU CALL A MAN STANDING BETWEEN TWO BLONDES?
A: An interpreter.

This guy wakes up out of a deep sleep and, feeling real horny, nudges his wife awake and asks, "Why don't we make love?"

She replies, "I have an appointment at the gynecologist tomorrow and I can't have sex the night before a physical exam."

So the husband grunts and rolls back over and starts to go back to sleep.

A few minutes later, he nudges his wife again and says, "You don't, by any chance, have a dentist's appointment tomorrow, do you?"

A guy goes to buy a train ticket, and the girl selling tickets has an incredible set of jugs. He can't take his eyes off them.

He says, "I'd like two pickets to Titsburgh . . . um . . . I mean, two tickets to Pittsburgh." He's incredibly embarrassed by the mistake.

The guy in line behind him says, "Relax, buddy. We all make Freudian slips like that. Just the other evening at dinner I meant to say to my wife, 'Please pass the butter,' but instead I said, 'You fucking bitch, you ruined my life.' "

**Q:** HOW DID THE MODEL HURT HERSELF RAKING LEAVES?
**A:** She fell out of the tree.

A man comes home to find his wife in the bedroom, her bags packed. "I'm going to Las Vegas," she announces. "I'm tired of asking you for money every week. There, they say, you can get $400 for a blow job."

He starts packing a suitcase, too.

"What are *you* doing?" his wife asks.

"I'm going, too. I want to see you try to live on $800 a year."

Three guys are applying for a job with the CIA. All three make it all the way to the final test.

The first guy walks into the director's office and sits down. The director reaches into his desk and pulls out a pistol. He lays it on his desk in front of the guy.

"This test is to test your loyalty," says the director. "Take this gun and go up the stairs and into the first room on your right. Your wife will be in there. Put a bullet in her head."

The guy looks at him and says, "No way."

So the director says, "I'm sorry. You fail."

The next guy comes in. The director tells him the same thing. This guy picks up the gun and heads for the room. He comes back about fifteen minutes later and tells the director that he just couldn't go through with it.

The director says, "I'm sorry. You fail."

The third guy comes in, and the director tells him the same thing. He heads up to the room. The director hears three shots, followed by a troubling series of crashes and clangs. The third guy comes back all beaten up and with his clothes all torn to shreds.

"What happened to you?" asks the director.

The guy replies, "After three shots, I realized that there were blanks in the gun, so I had to choke the bitch to death."

**Q:** WHAT'S EVEN DUMBER THAN A BLONDE TRYING TO BUILD A HOUSE IN A POND?

**A:** A jealous blonde trying to burn it down.

The night of their fiftieth wedding anniversary, a couple decided to have an elegant five-course dinner at home. Because it was a special night, they added a wrinkle—they would be naked.

During the first course, the man says to his wife, "Honey, my cock is as hungry for you as it was on our wedding night."

His wife replies, "Darling, my nipples are as hot for you as they ever have been."

"It makes sense," the husband says. "They're hanging in the soup."

**Q:** WHY DID GOD CREATE ADAM BEFORE EVE?

**A:** Because He didn't want anyone telling Him how to make Adam.

Sam is walking down the street after a sex-change operation has transformed him into a beautiful woman. An old friend sees him and says, "Sam, you look great . . . you're beautiful!"

Sam says, "Thanks . . . but holy Christ, did it hurt."

His friend says, "You mean when they cut open your chest and put in those implants?"

Sam says, "No, that didn't really hurt."

His friend says, "When they cut off your dick and put in a vagina?"

Sam says, "No, that didn't really hurt."

His friend says, "Then what hurt?"

Sam says, "When the doctor drilled a fucking hole in my head and sucked out half my brain."

Q: WHY DON'T BLONDES LIKE VIBRATORS?
A: They chip their teeth on them.

Q: HOW CAN YOU MAKE YOUR WIFE SCREAM DURING SEX?
A: Call her up and tell her about it.

After many months of trying to make ends meet, one New York City couple decide that the only way they are going to get by is to have the woman start hooking. So she dresses up and goes out on the streets.

Early the next morning, she comes home looking haggard and worn-out. The husband asks how she did, and the wife replies that she earned $400.20.

"That's great!" the husband says. "But who gave you the dimes?"

"Everybody!" replies the wife.

**Q:** How do you sink a submarine full of blondes?
**A:** Knock on the hatch.

Two guys sitting at a bar start talking about crime.

"It's getting bad," one of the guys says. "Someone stole my wife's credit card two months ago."

"How long did he have it before you called it in?" the other asks.

"Oh, I haven't called it in," the man replies. "He's spending less than my wife."

A man has tried to get his wife to blow him his entire married life, but she's never given in. He's tried again and again, but she's always turned him down.

He's begged and pleaded, but she's always insisted that she'd rather die a horrible, disfiguring death than do it. One night, the argument gets very heated, and after hours of screaming, yelling, crying, ranting, and raving, she finally agrees to go down on him.

She takes his penis in her hand and then slowly starts to put it in her mouth. Just as she gets her lips over the head, the phone rings, and he answers it.

He says, "Hello? Yes, she's home."

He looks down at her and says, "It's for you, cocksucker."

**Q:** Why do so many blondes have blue eyes?

**A:** They don't. That's the sky shining in from their ears.

**Q:** WHY DO WIVES CLOSE THEIR EYES DURING SEX?
**A:** They hate seeing their husbands having fun.

**Q:** WHAT'S THE DIFFERENCE BETWEEN YOUR PAYCHECK
AND YOUR COCK?
**A:** You don't have to beg your wife to blow your pay-
check!

A man comes home from a visit to the doctor with bad
news. He tells his wife that the doctor said he only has
thirty erections left in his life.

"Oh, my God," she says. "We'll have to think carefully
about when to use them."

"Yeah," he says. "I've made a list, but I don't think
you're on it."

**Q:** WHAT DOES THE BLONDE DO MOST MORNINGS?
**A:** Introduces herself and then walks home.

A gynecologist tells a woman she has acute vaginitis.

"Thanks," she replies, flattered.

**Q:** WHAT DO YOU CALL IT WHEN A BLONDE DIES HER
HAIR RED?
**A:** Artificial intelligence.

A farmer and his wife went to a fair. The farmer was fascinated by the airplanes and asked the pilot of an old-fashioned biplane how much a ride would cost.

"Ten dollars for three minutes," replied the pilot.

"That's too much," said the farmer.

The pilot thought for a second and then said, "I'll make you a deal. If you and your wife ride for three minutes without uttering a sound, the ride will be free. But if you make *any* sound, you'll have to pay ten dollars."

The farmer and his wife agreed and went for a wild ride. The pilot performed more than a few loops, spins, and dives. As they landed, the pilot shouted back to the farmer, "I want to congratulate you for not making a sound. You are a brave man."

"Perhaps," said the farmer. "But I gotta tell ya, I almost screamed when my wife fell out back there."

**Q:** WHAT DO YOU CALL A PARTICULARLY SMART
BLONDE?
**A:** A golden retriever.

Two guys are in a bar talking about their marriages. One says getting married was the best thing he ever did. The other says, "Oh, I definitely married Miss Right. I just didn't realize her first name was Always."

An angry wife met her husband at the door. There was alcohol on his breath and lipstick on his collar.

"I assume," she snarled, "that there is a very good reason for you to come stumbling in here at six o'clock in the morning, yes?"

"There is," he replied. "Breakfast."

The differences between a hooker, a girlfriend, and a wife:

"That's going to be another twenty dollars if you take any longer."

"Oh, baby, you're the best, you're the best!"

"Beige. I think I'll paint the ceiling beige."

Two guys are talking about sex, and both decide they like getting head best.

The first guy says to the second, "What's your favorite thing about a blow job?"

The second guy says, "Ten minutes of silence."

A man meets a woman at a bar and asks her, "Would you sleep with a man for a million dollars?"

"A million dollars?" she says. "Yes, I suppose I would."

"Great. Here's thirty-five dollars. Let's find a hotel room and go to bed."

"Thirty-five dollars?" the woman says. "What do you think I am?"

"We've already established that," he says. "Now we're just haggling over the price."

Q: WHAT DO YOU CALL A LINE OF WOMEN STANDING EAR TO EAR?
A: A wind tunnel.

A guy goes to a bar where he manages to pick up a gorgeous woman, and they go home together.

The next morning, while dressing, she sneers, "You didn't warn me you had such a small organ."

Annoyed, the guy replies, "And you didn't warn me I would be playing in such a large cathedral!"

Q: WHAT DO YOU CALL TWENTY MODELS IN A BLIZZARD?
A: Frosted Flakes.

A man at his wit's end is in his doctor's office asking for advice.

"Doctor, I can't break my wife of the habit of staying up until 5:00 A.M.," he says.

"What's she doing up till five o'clock?" asks the doctor.

"Waiting for me," the man replies.

A woman was riding a horse. It quickly increased its speed, and the woman fell back until she was only holding on by the tail. After a long struggle, she was able to climb back onto the horse. She then fell off the side and got her foot caught, so that the horse was now dragging her. She finally got back on the horse with a broken ankle, bruises all over, and bleeding from three different places. Finally, the horse came to a complete stop. Thank goodness that the manager of the Kmart had come out and shut the ride off!

One Sunday afternoon, a man was sitting in his lawn chair drinking beer and watching his wife mow the lawn.

A neighbor was so outraged at this, she walked across the street and said to the man, "You should be hung!"

"I am," he replied. "That's why she cuts the grass!"

A woman goes to see her doctor about a female problem. Her doctor says, "Are you sexually active?"

"No," she replies. "I just lie there."

Sally went to Nancy's place to tell her about a horrible experience she had the previous night with a guy she had taken home.

"Well, what happened when you got there?" asked Nancy.

"After we had sex, the son of a bitch called me a slut!"

Shocked, Nancy asked, "What did you do then?"

"I told him to get the hell out of my bedroom, and to take his eight friends with him!"

A model walks to a bank with a friend to cash a check. In front of the bank, she sees a sign that says 24-HOUR BANKING. She turns around and walks away.

"I just don't have that much time," she says to her friend.

Q: WHY DID THE BLONDE HAVE A BRUISE ON HER BELLY BUTTON?

A: Because her boyfriend was blond, too.

Two women are on opposite sides of a lake.

One yells, "How do you get to the other side?"

"You *are* on the other side," the other calls back.

A man was wandering around a supermarket, every now and again calling out, "Crisco! Crisco!"

Puzzled, a store clerk approached him.

"Sir, the Crisco is in aisle five."

"Sorry," replied the gentleman. "I'm not looking for cooking Crisco, I'm calling for my wife."

"Your wife is named Crisco?"

"Nah," he answered, "I only call her that when we come to the supermarket."

"Really? What do you call her when you are *not* in the supermarket?"

"Lard ass."

Q: WHY WAS THERE LIPSTICK ON THE BLONDE'S STEER-
   ING WHEEL?
A: She tried to blow the horn.

A guy walks into a bar and sits down. The guy's face is bruised and bleeding.

"What in the world happened to you?" asks the bartender.

He says, "Oh, I got in a fight with my girlfriend, and I called her a two-bit whore."

"Yeah?" says the bartender. "What did she do?"

"She hit me in the face with her bag of quarters."

One day a boy asked his dad, "What's the difference between a pussy and a cunt?"

His father thought for a minute and said, "Come with me."

He took his son to his mother's bedroom, where she was sleeping nude. "Son," he whispered, "see that brown, furry patch? That is a pussy."

The boy asked, "May I touch it to see how furry it is?"

"No!" replied his father. "That might wake up the cunt."

Q: WHY DID THE BLONDE PUT TGIF ON ALL OF HER SHIRTS?

A: It stands for "Tits Go In Front" and reminded her which way to put her blouses on.

A man walks into a bar one night. He goes up to the bar and asks for a beer.

"Certainly, sir, that'll be one cent," says the bartender.

"One penny!" exclaims the guy.

The barman replies, "Yes."

So the guy glances over at the menu, and he asks, "Could I have a nice juicy T-bone steak, with fries, peas, and a salad?"

"Certainly, sir," replies the bartender. "But all that comes to real money."

"How much?" inquires the guy.

"Nine cents," the barkeep replies.

"Nine cents!" exclaims the guy. "Where's the man who owns this place?"

The barman replies, "Upstairs with my wife."

The guy says, "What's he doing with your wife?"

The bartender says, "The same thing I'm doing to his business."

Q: WHAT DID THE BLONDE ASK FOR AT THE DOLLAR STORE?

A: A price check.

A bartender was trying to console a guy in the bar who'd just found his wife in bed with another man.

"Get over it, buddy," he said. "It's not the end of the world."

"It's all right for you to say," answered the guy. "But what if you came home one night and caught another man in bed with your wife?"

The bartender thought for a moment, and then said, "I'd break his cane and kick his Seeing Eye dog in the ass."

Q: WHAT DO YOU CALL A WOMAN WITH AN UNATTRACTIVE MAN?

A: A hostage.

A guy goes up to a women in a bar and says, "Would you like to dance?"

"No thanks, I don't like this song," the woman says. "But even if I did, I wouldn't dance with you."

"Huh?" the guy says. "You must have misunderstood me, I said you look fat in those pants."

A blonde at a party was telling her friend that she'd sworn off men for life.

"They lie, they cheat, and they're just no good," she moaned. "From now on, when I want sex, I'm going to use my vibrator."

"What happens when the batteries run out?" asked her friend.

"That's simple," replied the blonde. "I'll just fake an orgasm, as usual!"

A woman ran into the supermarket to pick up a few items. She headed for the express line, where the clerk was talking on the phone.

"Excuse me," she said. "I'm in a hurry. Could you check me out, please?"

The clerk looked her up and down, and smiled.

"Nice tits," he said.

Q: HOW DID THE BLONDE WIND UP IN THE HOSPITAL WITH TIRE MARKS ON HER BACK?

A: She crawled across the street on her stomach when the sign said DON'T WALK.

Two guys are in a bar discussing their sex lives. One guy says to the other, "How's your sex life, buddy?"

The other guy answers, "Not so good. Every time I have sex with my girlfriend, she loses interest halfway through it."

The first guy says, "Yeah, I know what you mean. I used to have the same problem, but I found a cure. I hid a starter pistol under the bed. When she started to run out of steam, I simply fired the starter pistol. It gave her such a fright that she got all excited, and couldn't get enough!"

The other guy says, "Hmm. I think I'll try it."

The next day they are back in the bar again. The first guy says, "How'd the starter pistol work for you?"

The other guy says, "Don't ask! Last night we were having a little sixty-nine. As usual, she lost interest halfway through, so I fired a starter pistol, just as you suggested."

The first guy says, "So what happened?"

The other guy says, "She bit my cock, crapped on my face, and a naked man ran out of the closet with his hands up!"

At a business lunch, a man is having trouble splitting a large check with an associate. He turns from his associate to whisper in his secretary's ear.

"If you had 50 percent of $3,500 plus 15 percent, how much would you take off?" he says.

"Everything but my earrings," she says.

A blonde desperate for money kidnaps a child and puts a ransom note in his pocket that says, "Leave $10,000 in an envelope in the trash can out front. Signed, The Blonde Kidnapper." Then she sends the kid home.

That afternoon, she finds an envelope filled with $10,000 and a note saying, "How could you do this to another blonde?"

An old man goes to a warlock to ask him if he can remove a curse he has been living with for the last forty years.

The warlock says, "Maybe, but first you will have to tell me the exact words that were used to put this curse on you."

Without hesitation, the old man says, "I now pronounce you man and wife."

Q: HOW MANY BLONDES DOES IT TAKE TO MAKE POP-CORN?
A: Four. One to hold the pan, and three to shake the stove.

A model discovers love letters from another woman in her boyfriend's apartment, confirming a suspicion she's had for a long time.

"I knew it!" she screamed, pulling a gun out of her

purse and pointing it at her head. "If I can't have you to myself, then I don't want to live!"

"Honey, for God's sake, don't do it!" the boyfriend screamed back.

"Oh, don't be so concerned about me," she said, tightening her grip on the trigger. "You're next!"

A man comes home from an exhausting day at work, plops down on the couch in front of the television, and tells his wife, "Get me a beer before it starts."

The wife sighs and gets him a beer. Fifteen minutes later, he says, "Get me another beer before it starts."

She looks cross, but fetches another beer and slams it down next to him. He finishes that beer and a few minutes later says, "Quick, get me another beer. It's going to start any minute."

The wife is furious. She yells at him, "Is that all you're going to do tonight? Drink beer and sit in front of that TV? You're nothing but a lazy, drunken, fat slob, and furthermore . . ."

The man sighs and says, "It's started."

Q: WHAT TRAGEDY RECENTLY TOOK PLACE IN A BASEBALL STADIUM?
A: When the crowd did the wave, two blondes drowned.

A blonde was complaining to a man she met in a bar about how women with light hair were stereotyped as being stupid.

"I'm not dumb," she said. "I know the capital of every state."

"Really?" the guys said. "What's the capital of Wisconsin?"

"That one's easy: *W.*"

A woman golfer called her pro to say that she couldn't keep her appointment for a lesson. The pro asked her why, and she explained that she had been stung by a bee while playing a round of golf.

"Where?" he asked.

"Between the first and second holes," she replied.

"Oh," her pro said. "I guess that would make it hard on your stance."

Q: WHY DO BLONDES TAKE VERY LONG SHOWERS?
A: All the shampoo bottles say, "Lather. Rinse. Repeat."

A model was telling a Polack joke to a priest when halfway through the priest interrupted her.

"Didn't you know that I'm Polish?" he says.

"I'm sorry," she replies. "Do you want me to start over and talk more slowly?"

The doctor takes an emergency call at 2:00 A.M.

"You have to come over right away," a frantic woman screams from the other end of the phone. "My son just swallowed a condom."

Before the doctor can say anything, the woman drops the phone and he can hear yelling in the background. Then the woman comes back to the phone.

"Never mind, Doctor," she says. "My husband found another one!"

**Q:** WHY DO BLOND NURSES TAKE RED MARKERS TO WORK WITH THEM?
**A:** Just in case they have to draw blood.

**Q:** WHAT DO MODELS AND COMPUTERS HAVE IN COMMON?
**A:** You don't appreciate either one until they go down on you.

A woman is at her doctor's office, and suddenly she shouts out, "Doctor, kiss me!"

The doctor looks at her and tells her he can't, that it would be ethically wrong. About fifteen minutes later the woman once again shouts out, "Doctor, please kiss me just once!"

Again he refuses. "I'm sorry," he says. "But that is very much against the Hippocratic oath."

Another fifteen minutes pass, and the woman pleads with the doctor, "Doctor, Doctor, please kiss me just once!"

"Look," he says, "I'm sorry. I just *cannot* kiss you. In fact, I probably shouldn't even be fucking you."

Q: WHAT DID THE BLONDE'S RIGHT LEG SAY TO HER LEFT LEG?
A: Nothing. They've never met.

Q: WHAT DID THE MODEL SAY TO HER DOCTOR WHEN HE TOLD HER SHE WAS PREGNANT?
A: Do you think it's mine?

A guy calls his wife from the emergency room. He tells her that his finger was cut off at the construction site where he had been working that day. .

"Oh no!" cries the woman. "The whole finger?"

"No, thank God," replies the guy. "The one next to it."

A bunch of people were enjoying happy hour at a local bar. One of them asked the others what time they went to bed on work nights.

"Well," said a blond woman, "if I'm not in bed by ten o'clock, I just go home."

An executive's blond secretary hung up the phone sobbing. The man came out of his office and asked what the matter was.

"I just found out my mother died."

"Oh my," the boss said. "I'm so sorry. Please take off as much time as you need."

"No," the woman said. "I'd rather be here, to take my mind off it."

The man nodded, then went back into his office. Ten minutes later, the phone rang again. This time, his secretary was wailing when she hung up.

"What's happened now?" the boss asked.

"Oh, I don't know if I can take it," the secretary responded. "That was my sister. Her mom's dead, too."

Q: WHAT DID THE MAN THINK WHEN HIS WIFE CAME HOME FROM THE DOCTOR'S AND REPORTED THAT THE DOCTOR TOLD HER SHE COULDN'T MAKE LOVE?
A: "I wonder how he found out?"

A blonde was in a cheese store and spied a tray of Gouda that said, "Free Samples."

She took a few, but found herself in a great deal of pain later that night.

She went back to the store the next day, wan and pale, and told the clerk, "Your cheese made me very sick last night!"

The clerk had obviously heard this from other customers.

"Well," he said, "what do you want us to do about that?"

"I want my money back!" she replied.

Q: WHAT IS THE DIFFERENCE BETWEEN A WOMAN AND AN INFLATABLE DOLL?
A: About two cans of hair spray.

A woman goes to see her doctor, who gives her a clean bill of health, except for some bruised, rough patches on her knees.

"I'm afraid those are from sexual activity," she explains to the doctor. "I do it doggy style a lot."

"Well," the doctor says, "I suggest you change that for a while. Do you know any other positions?"

"Sure," she says. "But my dog doesn't."

A blonde stops a man on a street and asks for the time.

"Three-seventeen," the man replies.

"Darn it," the blonde says, close to tears. "I've been asking people that question all day long, and I can't get anyone to agree."

Q: WHAT'S A REDHEAD'S MATING CALL?
A: "Has the blonde left yet?"

An attractive young girl, chaperoned by a very old woman, entered the doctor's office.

"We have come for an examination," said the girl.

"All right," said the doctor. "Go behind that curtain and take off all your clothes."

"No, not me," said the girl. "It's for my aunt."

"Very well," said the doctor. "Madam, stick out your tongue."

Q: WHY WAS THE BLONDE THE ONLY ONE ON THE BOAT SMILING DURING THE LIGHTNING STORM?
A: She thought her picture was being taken.

A woman goes into a store to buy a rod and reel. She doesn't know which one to get, so she just grabs one and goes over to the register. A salesman is standing there with dark shades on.

She says, "Excuse me, sir . . . can you tell me anything about this rod and reel?"

He says, "Ma'am, I'm blind, but if you will drop it on the counter, I can tell you everything about it from the sound it makes." She doesn't believe him, but drops it on the counter anyway.

He says, "That's a six-foot graphite rod with a Zyton 3003 reel and twenty-pound test line. It's a good deal for twenty dollars."

She says, "That's amazing! I think it's what I'm looking for, so I'll take it."

He walks behind the counter to the register, and in the meantime the woman farts. She's embarrassed, but she also figures the salesman won't know who it was, since he's blind.

He rings up the sale and says, "That will be $25.50."

She says, "But didn't you say it was $20?"

He says, "Yes, ma'am, the rod and reel is $20, the duck call is $3, and the catfish stink bait is $2.50."

It was the first day of the school year, and an elementary-school teacher was trying to get to know her students.

"What did you do this summer?" the teacher asked Suzie.

"My family and I went to the beach a lot," Suzie answered.

"That sounds like fun," said the teacher. "How about you, Emma? What did you do this summer?"

"My family and I rode our bikes together."

"That sounds lovely," said the teacher. She continued with all her pupils until she got to Timmy in the corner of the room.

"What did you do this summer, Timmy?"

"Nothing," the boy responded timidly.

"Didn't you do anything with your family?" the teacher asked, trying to draw Timmy out.

"Yes."

"Did you go to the beach?"

"No."

"Did you ride bikes?"

"Never!" the boy yelled. "We *never* ride bikes together!"

"Why not?" said the teacher.

"I don't know," explained Timmy. "But my dad says that when my mom and my sisters are cycling together, he has to get the hell out of town."

**Q:** HOW DO YOU DEFINE *ETERNITY?*
**A:** Four blond drivers at a four-way stop.

A man gets on an elevator and is quickly pushed to the rear by everyone else getting on.

"Ballroom, please," he says to the elevator operator.

A woman standing in front of him turns around and says, "I'm sorry, I didn't realize I was crowding you."

One Friday afternoon, Ethel and Shirley are sitting in Ethel's living room. Ethel looks out the window and sees her husband, Herb, walking toward the house carrying a bouquet of flowers.

Ethel says, "Uh-oh. Here comes Herb with a bunch of

flowers. That means I'll be on my back with my legs up in the air all weekend."

"Why on earth would you do that?" says Shirley. "Haven't you got a vase?"

**Q:** WHY WAS THE BLONDE FOUND DEAD IN THE PARKING LOT OF A MINNESOTA DRIVE-IN MOVIE THEATER?
**A:** She went to see *Closed for the Winter*.

Three women at a party were talking about their love lives.

The first said, "My husband is like a Mercedes; smooth and sophisticated."

The second said, "Mine is like a BMW; fast and powerful."

The third said, "Mine is like an old Ford. It needs a hand start and I have to jump on quickly while it's still going."

A guy walks into an elevator and stands next to a beautiful woman. After a few minutes, he turns to her and says, "Can I smell your pussy?"

The woman looks at him in disgust and says, "Certainly not!"

"Hmm," he replies. "It must be your feet, then."

**Q:** HOW MANY BLONDES DOES IT TAKE TO CHANGE A LIGHTBULB?

**A:** Seven. One to hold the bulb, two to hold the ladder, and four to turn the house.

On their fiftieth wedding anniversary, Helen and Bob are sharing a candlelit dinner when Bob asks a question he's been thinking about for years.

"Helen," he says. "Be honest. Have you ever cheated on me?"

"Well, yes," she confesses. "But only three times."

"Three?" Bob says. "I guess that isn't bad for fifty years. When were they?"

"Remember forty-one years ago, when you really needed that bank loan to start your business, and the bank president finally changed his mind and gave you the money?"

"Oh, Helen," Bob says. "You did that for me!"

"Yes," she continues. "And remember when you were trying to land that big account from St. Louis twenty years ago, and the sales executive suddenly signed up with you?"

"Oh, Helen," Bob says again. "You were there for me!"

"And remember three months ago, when you were up for country-club president, and only needed thirty-four votes?"

A lesbian goes to a gynecologist, and after examining her, the doctor says, "I must say, this is the cleanest pussy I've seen ever."

"Thanks," said the lesbian. "I have a woman in four times a week."

Q: HOW DID THE BLOND COYOTE WIND UP WITH ONE LEG?

A: She got it stuck in a trap and chewed off the other three.

A man approaches an attractive woman in the meat department of a large supermarket. "I'm afraid I've lost my wife here in the supermarket," he says. "Can you talk to me for a couple of minutes?"

"Why?" she asks.

"Because every time I talk to a beautiful woman, she appears out of nowhere," he replies.

Two elderly women are sitting on their front porch.

One turns to the other and asks, "Do you still get horny?"

The other replies, "Oh, I sure do."

The first one asks, "What to you do about it?"

The second replies, "I suck on a Life Saver."

After a few moments, the first one asks, "Who drives you to the beach?"

**Q:** If a blonde and a brunette jump off a building, who will be the first to reach the ground?

**A:** The brunette. The blonde will have to stop to ask for directions.

Getting married is very much like going to a restaurant with a friend. You order what you want, and then when you see what the other person has, you want *that* instead.

A woman goes into a sporting-goods store and says to the salesman, "I need a present for my son's birthday tomorrow."

The salesman says, "How old is he?"

The customer says, "He's twelve."

He says, "How about this skateboard?"

She says, "How much is it?"

He says, "$79.95."

She says, "That's too much."

The salesman says, "How about this baseball bat?"

The customer says, "How much is that?"

He says, "$14.95."

She says, "All right, I'll take it."

The salesman says, "Do you wanna ball for the bat?"

The customer thinks for a minute, then says, "No, but I'll blow you for the skateboard."

**Q:** WHAT DO YOU CALL TWO OLDER BLONDES IN THE FRONT SEAT OF A CAR?

**A:** Dual air bags.

In the midst of a marital fight, a wife tells her husband, "You know I was an idiot when I married you."

"I know," the husband replies. "But I was in love and didn't notice."

A blonde was having sex with her boyfriend one night when she said, "Just tonight, could you put it in the other hole? I really, really like that."

And her boyfriend said, "What? And risk getting you pregnant?"

**Q:** WHAT'S THE DIFFERENCE BETWEEN A BLOND MAN AND A BLOND WOMAN?

**A:** The woman has a much higher sperm count.

Man is incomplete until he is married. Only then is he finished.

A woman is returning a CD player she bought from a store. She has the receipt and the original packaging.

"Ma'am," the manager says, "it's our policy that we charge you a 35 percent restocking fee for a returned item."

"Feel my tits!" she suddenly cries. "Quick—feel my tits!"

Surprised, the manager nonetheless grabs her chest and says, "For God's sake, why?"

"I like guys to feel my tits when I'm getting screwed," she says.

Q: WHY DON'T BLONDES HAVE ANY ICE IN THE FREEZER?
A: They keep forgetting how to make it.

A young man asks his father, "How much does it cost to get married?"

Dad answers, "I'll tell you when I die."

Q: THERE ARE TWO GUYS, ONE IN A CIRCUS AND THE OTHER IN A BEDROOM. ONE IS WALKING A TIGHTROPE, AND THE OTHER IS GETTING A BLOW JOB FROM A NINETY-YEAR-OLD WOMAN. WHAT ARE BOTH OF THEM THINKING?
A: "Don't look down."

Q: WHY DO SO MANY BLONDES DRIVE BMWs?
A: Because it's easy to spell.

Two women are gabbing over lunch in an expensive restaurant.

"You know, I made my third husband a millionaire."

"Really? What was he before?"

"A billionaire."

A guy goes to a whorehouse. He selects a girl, pays her $200, and gets undressed. She's about to take off her clothes when the fire alarms sounds. She runs out of the room, with his $200 still in her hand. He quickly grabs his clothes and runs after her. He searches the building, but the smoke gets so heavy, he runs outside looking for her. By this time, there are three fire trucks and more than thirty firemen there.

Stopping one of them, he says, "Did you see a beautiful blonde with $200 in her hand?"

The fireman says, "No!"

So the guy says, "Well, if you see her, fuck her. It's already paid for."

A blonde peels off the top of a game token in a diner and starts screaming, "I won a motor home! I won a motor home!"

The others are surprised that the promotion brought such high stakes. The manager comes out, and also looks skeptical. He asks to see the token, then reads it back to the blonde.

"Ma'am, it says: 'Win a Bagel.'"

One evening in a beautiful French restaurant, a woman drew her husband's attention to a couple at a table nearby.

"Do you see those two?" she said. "Do you see how devoted they are? He kisses her every few minutes, as though they haven't seen each other in months. Why don't you do that?"

"I would love to," replied the husband. "But I don't know her well enough."

A man and his wife are fucking vigorously, and sweating profusely all the while. Fifteen minutes pass, then thirty minutes, and then an hour, and they're still going at it!

The woman finally opens her eyes and says, "What's the matter, darling, can't you think of anyone else, either?"

You know the honeymoon is pretty much over when you start to go out with the boys on Thursday nights, and so does she.

Q: WHAT GOES:

   blonde

   brunette

blonde

brunette

blonde

brunette

blonde

brunette

**A:** A blonde doing cartwheels.

A man wandering around a carnival sees a booth with a sign that says KISSES: $5 TO $50.

He asks the girl, "Does the price depend on how long the kiss is?"

"No," she says, "it depends on where I kiss you."

**Q:** WHAT DID THE MAN DO WHEN HIS GIRLFRIEND TOLD HIM HE SHOULD BE MORE AFFECTIONATE?

**A:** He got *two* girlfriends.

A blonde is on a date, and they drive up to Lovers' Point. They're going at it in the front seat, and the guy can tell she's ready. "Do you want to go in the backseat?" he asks.

"No!" she replies.

So they continue where they are, even though it's uncomfortable, and he quickly takes her shirt off.

"You want to go in the backseat now?" he asks.

"Of course not!" she says.

After another five minutes, he's got her pants off, too, and he figures she must be ready now.

"Ready for the backseat?" he asks again.

"I don't want to go in the backseat!" she cries. "I want to stay up here with you."

**Q:** WHAT IS DUMBER THAN TWO GUYS BUILDING A BRIDGE IN A DESERT?

**A:** Two blondes trying to fish off it.

Becky was on her deathbed, and her loyal husband, Dale, sat by her side.

"Dale, I must confess," she said at last. "I cheated on you years ago, on our wedding night."

"Oh, Becky, don't say another word about it," he replied.

"There's more. I gambled away our savings on the slots. It's all gone."

"Oh, Becky, don't say another word about it."

"And I've been having affairs with your partner, Bob; your brother, Charles; and the gardener and the plumber."

"Oh, Becky, don't say another word about it. I know all this already. That's why I poisoned you."

**Q:** WHY ARE BLOND WOMEN SO STUPID?

**A:** To make brunettes feel better about themselves.

Blonde Invention Number 679: dehydrated water.

One guy says to another in the office where they both work, "I've got a terrible headache, I think I'm going to leave early today."

"The same thing happened to me last week," the second guy says. "But I went home at lunch, banged my wife, and came back feeling great. You should try it."

"Wow," the first guy says in amazement. "I didn't even realize you knew I was banging your wife!"

A blonde was driving home when she saw a sign: CLEAN RESTROOMS, EIGHT MILES.

"Wow," she said, "isn't it lucky I already have a toilet brush in the trunk?"

Q: WHY DID THE BLONDE QUIT HER JOB AS A RESTROOM ATTENDANT?
A: She couldn't figure out how to refill the hand dryer.

Two guys in a bar are talking about their wives.

"My wife is pissed off at me again," says the first.

"Why?" says the second.

"I was bombed at the bar across the street last night," the first says. "And she came looking for me."

"What'd you do?" says the second.

"I asked her for her phone number," replies the first.

A cop pulls over a blond driver for going the wrong way on a one-way street.

"Where are you going?" he asks.

"I don't know, but I was having second thoughts about it," she says. "Everyone else was leaving."

Q: WHY DO MEN FART MORE THAN WOMEN?
A: Because women won't shut up long enough to build up the necessary pressure.

A police officer, though scheduled for all-night duty at the station, was relieved early and arrived home four hours ahead of schedule, at 2:00 A.M. Not wanting to wake his wife, he undressed in the dark, crept into the bedroom, and started to climb into bed. Just then his wife sat up.

"Charlie," she said. "Would you go down to the all-night drugstore and get me some aspirin? I've got a splitting headache."

"Certainly, honey," he said. He felt around in the dark for his badge and uniform, got dressed, and walked to the drugstore.

When he arrived, the pharmacist looked at him in surprise.

"I know you," said the druggist. "Aren't you the cop? Officer O'Rourke, right?"

"Yes," said the officer.

"Well, what are you doing dressed in the fire chief's uniform?" said the pharmacist.

A blonde and a brunette are taking skydiving lessons. The blonde jumps first, her parachute opens, and she glides toward earth. The brunette jumps second, but her parachute doesn't open. She opens her emergency chute, and that doesn't work either, so she goes plummeting past the blonde, screaming.

"So you want to race, huh?" the blonde yells back, unfastening her parachute.

**Q:** WHY DID THE BLONDE CLIMB THE GLASS WALL?
**A:** To see what was on the other side.

Doris and Betty, two old-maid roommates, are spending another lonely Saturday night together.

"I can't take it anymore," says Betty finally. "I'm going out and I'm not coming back until someone takes away my virginity."

She comes back at dawn, staggering inside.

"Betty, what happened!" says Doris.

"You're not going to believe it," Betty says. "It was ten inches when it went in, and five inches when it came out. When I find the rest of it, Doris, you and I are going to have the time of our lives."

Q: WHY ARE BLONDE WOMEN ONLY ALLOWED TO TAKE FIFTEEN-MINUTE LUNCH BREAKS?

A: Otherwise, they have to be retrained.

Q: WHAT DID THE BLONDE YELL OUT WHEN SHE WITNESSED A CAR CRASH?

A: "What's the number for 911?"

A man comes home with his daughter, whom he has just taken to the office for "Take Our Daughters to Work" day.

The little girl says, "When you talk to your secretary, why do you call her a doll?"

Feeling his wife's gaze upon him, the man explains, "Well, honey, my secretary is a very hardworking girl. She types like you wouldn't believe, she knows computers, and is very efficient."

"Oh. I thought it was because she closes her eyes when you lay her down on the couch."

Q: HOW DO YOU BRAINWASH A BLONDE?

**A:** Give her a douche, turn her upside down, and shake her.

**Q:** WHY DO THEY GIVE FEMALE NAMES TO HURRICANES?
**A:** When they come, they're all wet and wild. When they leave, your house is gone.

A son asks his father, "What's the difference between *hypothetical* and *realistic?*"

The dad explains: "Go ask your sister if she would have sex with Charlie next door for $500,000, then ask your mom if she would screw the mailman for $500,000."

The boy goes off and soon comes back.

"Sis said, 'Hell yeah,' and Mom said, 'Of course.' "

"There you have it," his father says. "Hypothetically, we're millionaires. But realistically, we're just living with a couple of whores."

**Q:** HOW DO THEY MEASURE A BLONDE'S IQ?
**A:** Insert a tire gauge in her ear.

**Q:** WHY DID THE WOMAN CROSS THE ROAD?
**A:** She crossed the road? What the hell is she doing out of the kitchen?

A blonde, a brunette, and a redhead all went into the OB-GYN office together. When they met after their checkups, the redhead was smiling, and the brunette asked her why. "I'm going to have a baby boy," the redhead replied.

"How do you know?" asked the blonde.

"Because I was on top."

This got the brunette thinking, and she smiled as well. "I'm having a girl!" she said proudly.

The blonde asked how she knew.

"I was on bottom," said the brunette.

The blonde started to heave and cry.

"Why are you crying?" both of the others asked.

"Because I'm going to have puppies!" the blonde replied in tears.

Q: HOW DOES A BLONDE TRY TO KILL FISH?
A: She drowns them.

Q: HOW MANY WOMEN DOES IT TAKE TO CHANGE A LIGHTBULB?
A: Six. One to talk to her friends about how she's going to do it, and the five friends to say her boyfriend should do it.

Q: WHAT DOES A BLONDE SAY WHEN SHE SEES A BANANA
PEEL ON THE SIDEWALK?
A: "Uh-oh. I'm going to fall again."

Q: WHY IS A BLONDE'S COFFIN Y-SHAPED?
A: Because as soon as she is on her back, her legs open.

A TV producer was interviewing a young model.

He asked, "If you could have a conversation with anyone, living or dead, who would it be?"

The model thought for a minute, then replied, "The living one."

Q: WHAT'S THE DIFFERENCE BETWEEN LOVE, TRUE
LOVE, AND SHOWING OFF?
A: Spitting, swallowing, and gargling.

Q: WHY DON'T BLOND WOMEN WORK AS ELEVATOR
ATTENDANTS?
A: They have to keep asking for directions.

A man decides to buy a pony for his daughter, so he goes out to a pony farm to get one. He agrees on a price of a dollar per pound with the farmer, and then he walks to the barn to select a pony.

"How about this one?" he says to the farmer, pointing to a young one.

"Okay," says the farmer.

The farmer then picks up the pony, puts its tail in his mouth, lets it hang there briefly, and then declares, "This one weighs seventy-four pounds."

"That's amazing," the man says. "Can you really tell a pony's weight by using that method?"

"Sure," replies the farmer. "We've used this method in our family for generations."

To prove it, the farmer puts the pony on a scale and it weighs exactly seventy-four pounds. "My son can do it, too," he boasts.

And sure enough, the farmer's son comes over, puts another pony's tail in his mouth, lets it hang, and then says, "This one weighs eighty-three pounds."

Then the farmer confirms his son's accuracy with the scale.

"My wife can do it, too," says the farmer. "Son, go get your mother."

The boy runs off to the house and comes back a few minutes later.

"Mom can't come out right now," says the son. "She's busy weighing the mailman."

Q: How do you keep a model busy for hours?

**A:** Give her a piece of paper with the same thing on both sides: "Instructions on Back."

**Q:** WHAT'S THE DIFFERENCE BETWEEN AND A BLONDE AND A BROOM CLOSET?

**A:** Only two guys can get inside a broom closet at once.

A farmer's wife calls the vet to come take a look at her cow.

"Doctor," she says. "My cow seems to become sad every time I milk her."

"Sure," the vet says. "How would you feel if someone rubbed your tits every morning for two hours without fucking you?"

A model walks into a winter clothing store. She picks out a scarf and takes it to the counter to pay for it. When she gets home, she turns around and takes it right back to the store. The clerk asks why she's returning the scarf.

"Because," she says, "it's too tight!"

**Q:** HOW DOES A BLONDE GET PREGNANT?

**A:** Hey, they're not that dumb.

**Q:** WHY DO UGLY GIRLS LIKE TRICK-OR-TREATING BETTER THAN SEX?

**A:** On Halloween, the uglier you are, the easier it is to get some.

There were nine blondes and one brunette hanging off of a sheer cliff on a rope. The rope could only hold nine people, so one person would have to let go and sacrifice her life so the rest would survive. The brunette offers a heartwarming speech saying that she'll give her life for the others, that she'll let go and fall.

When she finishes speaking, the blondes are so moved that they all begin to applaud.

**Q:** HOW DO YOU DROWN A BLONDE?

**A:** Put a mirror at the bottom of a pool.

**Q:** HOW ELSE DO YOU DROWN A BLONDE?

**A:** Put a scratch-and-sniff book at the bottom of the pool.

An old woman went to visit her daughter and she found her naked, waiting for her husband.

"What are you doing naked?" says the mother.

"This is my love dress," the daughter says.

142

When the mother returns home, she strips naked and waits for her husband.

When her husband arrives, he asks her, "What are you doing naked?"

"This is my love dress," she says in a husky voice.

"Well," he replies. "Go iron it."

**Q:** WHAT DID THE BLONDE SAY WHEN SHE WENT INTO THE ANTIQUE SHOP?

**A:** "What's new?"

A guy goes to his high-school reunion. Not having seen anyone in thirty years, he's very curious about who might turn up. When he gets there, he runs into his old high-school girlfriend. They sit down and talk about the past.

"How have you been?" he asks.

"I've been fine, just fine," she replies. "Although I do have some good news and some bad news."

"Bad news first," he says.

"Well, a few weeks ago I had to have a hysterectomy," she replies.

"Oh, that's terrible," he says. "I'm sorry to hear that."

"But the good news is," she continues, "the doctor found the high-school class ring you thought you lost!"

**Q:** WHAT HAPPENED WHEN THE BLONDE BOUGHT AN AM RADIO?

**A:** It took her two months to figure out she could play it at night!

**Q:** WHAT JOB DID THE M&M PLANT MANAGER GIVE HIS BLOND GIRLFRIEND?
**A:** Proofreader.

A wife figured out her husband was having an affair with the hot young thing across the street, and it really annoyed her when she awoke alone early one Sunday morning.

She called over there, and the woman answered the phone.

"Tell my husband to get his ass across the street," said the wife.

"Honey," the other woman replied. "He's been doing that for three months now."

**Q:** WHY DON'T MODELS EVER DOUBLE RECIPES?
**A:** Because their ovens won't go over 750 degrees.

**Q:** WHAT DO YOU CALL A BLONDE WHO LOSES 90 PERCENT OF HER BRAINS?
**A:** Divorced.

A note on a condom vending machine in a men's room read: "If this machine doesn't work, see the bar manager. If it does, see the barmaid."

The model was complaining to one of her friends about the previous evening.

"It was terrible!" she said. "I had to change seats five times at the movie last night!"

"Did some guy bother you?" said her friend.

"Yeah. Eventually."

Q: WHAT DO YOU CALL THREE PROSTITUTES AND A BLONDE?

A: Ho, Ho, Ho, and to all a good night.

Mickey and Minnie are in divorce court.

The judge asks Mickey, "Let me get this straight. You're divorcing Minnie because she's insane?"

"No, Your Honor," replies Mickey. "I'm divorcing her because she's fucking Goofy!"

There was this model, and her house was on fire. She called the fire department to report the fire. Annoyed when the dispatcher asked how to get to her house, she replied, "Duh . . . Use the big red truck!"

**Q:** HOW CAN YOU TELL WHEN A FAX IS FROM A BLONDE?
**A:** There's a stamp on it.

As the young couple parked in a crowded lovers' lane, she sighed romantically. "It's lovely out here tonight," she said. "Just listen to those crickets."

"Those aren't crickets," her boyfriend said. "They're zippers."

**Q:** WHAT HAPPENED TO THE MODEL WHO GOT LOCKED IN A BATHROOM?
**A:** She peed in her pants.

**Q:** WHICH BLONDES WRITE MYSTERIES?
**A:** The ones with checkbooks.

A sixteen-year-old girl went to a boutique and bought a teeny tiny bikini. Proudly, she came home and tried it on. Then she went to show her mother how she looked in it.

"What do you think, Mom?" she asked.

Her mother replied: "If I had worn that when I was your age, you'd be six years older."

146

A man visiting his uncle's grave can't help but stare at another man not far away, crying uncontrollably before a tombstone, pounding the earth, and screaming toward the sky.

"Why did you have to die? Why did you have to die?" he's wailing.

Concerned, the first man walks over.

"May I ask who you are mourning? A lost parent? A child? A cherished sibling?" he gently asks.

"No," the man replies, disconsolate. "My wife's first husband!"

**Q:** WHY DO WOMEN HAVE TROUBLE ACHIEVING ORGASM?
**A:** Do you care?

**Q:** WHAT DOES A BLONDE SAY AFTER MULTIPLE ORGASMS?
**A:** "Way to go, team!"

**Q:** HOW DOES A MODEL KILL A BIRD?
**A:** By throwing it off a cliff.

**Q:** WHY DID THE YOUNG BLONDE HAVE SQUARE BOOBS?
**A:** She didn't take the tissues out of the box.

Worried about their listless love life, a young wife sent her husband to a sex hypnotist. Soon everything got much better. But she couldn't help noticing that each night, in the middle of the sex act, her husband would dash out to the bathroom for several minutes. This tormented her until finally, one night, she followed him to the bathroom. There, in front of the mirror, she watched him swinging a pocket watch in front of his eyes and whispering: "She's not my wife . . . she's not my wife . . . she's not my wife . . ."

"What's the matter, ma'am?" asked the maid, finding her employer in tears.

"I've just discovered my husband is having an affair with his secretary!" the woman cried.

"Nonsense!" snorted the maid. "You're only saying that to make me jealous!"

Q: WHY DO BLONDES HAVE ORGASMS?
A: So they know when to stop having sex.

Q: WHAT'S THE ONLY THING THAT WILL MAKE FIVE POUNDS OF FAT LOOK BEAUTIFUL?
A: A nipple.

An old couple are sitting on the porch one afternoon rocking in their rocking chairs. All of a sudden the old man reaches over and slaps his wife.

Shocked, she says, "What on earth was that for?"

He says, "That's for thirty years of rotten sex!"

She says nothing and they begin rocking again.

Suddenly she reaches over and slaps her husband.

He says, "What was that for?"

She says, "That's for knowing the difference!"

Q: WHY DON'T BLONDES BREAST-FEED?
A: They keep burning their nipples.

A hunter is stalking a deer in the woods when he comes to a clearing. There, tied to a tree, is a beautiful woman, stark naked.

"Oh, thank heavens!" she says. "Three men brought me here, ripped my clothes off, tied me to this tree, had their way with me, and then just *left* me here! Thank God you've rescued me!"

"Lady," says the hunter, unbuckling his belt, "this just isn't your day . . ."

Q: WHAT'S THE WORST THING ABOUT SEX WITH TEENAGE GIRLS?
A: Bucket seats.

**Q:** WHAT TWO THINGS IN THE AIR CAN GET A WOMAN PREGNANT?

**A:** Her feet.

A man comes home to find his wife in bed with the neighbor.

"You were right, honey," the husband tells her. "He *is* cheating on his wife."

**Q:** SANTA CLAUS, THE EASTER BUNNY, A DUMB BLONDE, AND A SMART BLONDE ARE ALL WALKING DOWN THE STREET WHEN THEY SPOT A TEN-DOLLAR BILL. WHO PICKS IT UP?

**A:** The dumb blonde. She's the only one that exists.

Correction:

**A:** Actually, none of them does. The dumb blonde thought it was a gum wrapper.

A man went to the perfume counter in a department store and asked to see their best. The clerk showed the man the most expensive scent they carried.

"This is called Perhaps," said the salesclerk. "It's $285 an ounce."

"Listen," the man said. "For $285 an ounce, I don't want something called Perhaps, I want something called You Can Bet Your Goddamn Ass on It."

A man had six children and was very proud of his achievement. He was so pleased with himself that he started calling his wife "Mother of Six," although she hated the nickname. One night at a party, the man repeatedly referred to her as "Mother of Six," despite all the odd looks it caused. As the night ended, he shouted across the room, "Shall we go home, Mother of Six?"

His wife called back: "Anytime you're ready, Father of Four!"

Q: WHAT'S THE DIFFERENCE BETWEEN A BLONDE AND THE *TITANIC?*
A: They know how many men went down on the *Titanic.*

Two blondes were driving through the Deep South. As they were approaching the town of Natchitoches, they started arguing about the pronunciation of the name. The argument went on until they stopped for lunch.

As they stood at the counter, one blonde asked the manager, "Before we order, could you please settle an argument? Would you please pronounce where we are, very slowly?"

The manager leaned over the counter and said, "Burrrrrrrr-gerrrrrrr Kiiiiing."

A couple in their late thirties were getting ready to go to bed. Right before climbing in, the man took off his glasses.

"You know, honey," the wife said, "without those glasses on, you look like the same handsome young man I married fifteen years ago."

"Without these glasses," he replied. "You look halfway decent, too."

Q: WHAT DID THE BLONDE SAY TO HER DATE AFTER HE BLEW IN HER EAR?
A: Thanks for the refill.

"Darn it!" the blonde said. "I just can't get this tiger puzzle together."

"Honey," her boyfriend said. "Please put the Frosted Flakes back in the box."

A man is reading the paper when he sees an ad for a big sale on tires.

"Look at this! Four tires for ninety dollars."

His wife snorts and says, "What do you care? We don't even have a car."

"So?" he replies. "I don't give you a hard time for going bra shopping, do I?"

**Q:** WHY DO BRIDES SMILE WALKING DOWN THE AISLE?
**A:** They know they've given their last blow job.

**Q:** HOW WOULD A BLONDE PUNCTUATE THE FOLLOWING: FUN FUN FUN WORRY WORRY WORRY?
**A:** Here's how: fun period fun period fun no period worry worry worry.

There once was a woman who had nineteen children. She loved them all, but—as you can imagine—found it hard to look after all nineteen. Eventually, the stress proved too much for her and she died. At her funeral, the priest said, "Now, finally, they're back together, as they should be."

"What do you mean?" asked her widower after the service. "The kids and I are still alive—all twenty of us!"

"No," the priest replied. "I meant her legs."

**Q:** WHY DID THE BLONDE PUT CONDOMS ON HER EARS?
**A:** So she wouldn't get Hearing AIDS.

Q: WHY DID GOD GIVE MAN A PENIS?
A: So there'd be at least one way to shut up a woman.

Q: WHY DID THE WOMAN COMPLAIN AFTER GETTING HER
   DRIVER'S LICENSE?
A: She thought she deserved an A in sex.

Q: WHY IS A WOMAN'S BRAIN THE SIZE OF A PEA AFTER
   EXERCISING?
A: It swells up.

An older woman goes to the doctor to ask his help in re-
viving her husband's sex drive. She had suggested Viagra
to him, but he refused to take any medication for any reason—even a headache.

"No problem," replies the doctor. "Drop Viagra into his
coffee, and he won't even taste it. Try it and come back in
a week to let me know how it worked."

A week later she returns to the doctor, and he asks
how things went. "Oh, it was terrible, Doctor, just terrible."

"What happened?" asks the doctor.

"Well, I did as you suggested and slipped the Viagra in
his coffee. The effect was immediate. He jumped straight
up, swept everything off the table, ripped all my clothes

off, and proceeded to make passionate love to me right there on the tabletop. It was just terrible."

"What was terrible?" asked the doctor. "Wasn't the sex any good?"

"Oh, Doctor, the sex was the best I've had in twenty-five years, but I'll never be able to show my face in Mc-Donald's again."

Q: WHAT DO YOU CALL A BLONDE DOING A HANDSTAND?
A: A brunette.

Q: WHAT IS PARTICULARLY LONG AND HARD FOR MOST WOMEN?
A: Fourth grade.

A woman's car broke down. A cop pulled up and asked her what the group of naked men next to her were doing.

"They're my emergency flashers," she explained.

A model is driving home one evening and decides to try something new, so she pulls into the video store to rent a porno tape. She chooses the title she likes best, rents it, and goes home. She puts on something comfortable and inserts the video into her VCR. To her disappointment, there's nothing but static on the tape, so she calls the store and explains what happened. The clerk asks her the name of the tape, and she says, *"Head Cleaner."*

Q: WHAT DID THE WOMAN ASK THE PROFESSOR DURING A LECTURE ON NUCLEAR FISSION?
A: What do you use for bait?

A woman walked into a gas station and told the manager, "I locked my keys in my car and I was wondering if you had a coat hanger I could stick through the window and unlock the door."

"Why, sure," said the manager. "We have a wire that works well for that."

A couple of minutes later, the manager walked outside to see how the woman was doing. He heard another voice. "No, no, a little to the left," said the other woman inside the car.

Q: WHAT'S BETTER THAN SEEING A WOMAN WRESTLE?
A: Seeing her box.

Q: WHAT DID THE MODEL DO AFTER READING THAT 90 PERCENT OF ALL ACCIDENTS OCCUR IN THE HOME?
A: She moved.

The epitome of laziness: a guy in California lying on top of a girl and waiting for an earthquake to do the rest.

**Q:** WHAT'S HALF A MILE LONG AND HAS AN IQ OF 126?
**A:** A parade of blonde women.

A woman ordered a pizza and the counterman asked if he should cut it in six or twelve pieces.

She responded, "Six, please. I could never eat twelve."

A prostitute tells a man she'll be charging him an extra $500 because she is a virgin. The man only has $100, but agrees to send her a check for the full amount. So no one gets suspicious, he says he'll mark the check "Rent."

Later, the man decides he has been overcharged. He sends along a $250 check and a note saying, "You said the apartment had never been used, but I could tell it had, and it was much bigger than advertised."

A week later, he received a note from the woman saying, "It's a shame you just didn't have enough furniture to fill it."

**Q:** WHAT DID THE WOMAN SAY WHEN HER BOYFRIEND TOLD HER HE WAS GOING SKEET SHOOTING?

**A:** But I don't even know how to cook those!

A young model was on vacation deep in Louisiana. She wanted a pair of genuine alligator shoes in the worst way, but was very reluctant to pay the high prices the local vendors were asking.

After becoming very frustrated with the "no haggle" attitude of one of the shopkeepers, the model shouted, "Maybe I'll just go out and catch my own alligator so I can get a pair of shoes at a reasonable price!"

The shopkeeper said, "By all means, be my guest. Maybe you'll luck out and catch yourself a big one!" Determined, the model turned and headed for the swamps, set on catching an alligator.

Driving home later that day, the shopkeeper spots the young woman standing waist-deep in the water, shotgun in hand. Just then, he sees a huge nine-foot alligator swimming quickly toward her. She takes aim, kills the creature, and with a great deal of effort hauls it onto the swamp bank. Lying nearby are several more of the dead creatures. The shopkeeper watches in amazement. Just then the model flips the alligator on its back, and frustrated, shouts out, "Damn it, this one isn't wearing any shoes either!"

**Q:** WHAT'S THE DIFFERENCE BETWEEN A WOMAN AND A WASHING MACHINE?

**A:** You can drop your load in a washing machine without its following you around all week.

**Q:** WHAT DID THE PROMISCUOUS WOMAN REFER TO AS HER "LOVE HANDLES"?

**A:** Her ears.

**Q:** WHAT DO TURTLES AND WOMEN HAVE IN COMMON?

**A:** If they're on their backs, they're screwed!

**Q:** WHAT DID THE BANANA SAY TO THE VIBRATOR?

**A:** What are you shaking for? I'm the one she's going to eat!

In a passionate and intimate moment, a woman says to her boyfriend, "Fuck my brains out!"

"I'm afraid it's too late," he replies.

**Q:** WHY DID THE WOMAN GET FIRED FROM HER JOB AS A QUALITY-CONTROL INSPECTOR AT THE M&M FACTORY?

**A:** She threw away all the "W&Ws."

**Q:** WHAT DO A WOMAN AND A CONDOM HAVE IN COMMON?

**A:** If they're not on your dick, they're in your wallet.

A woman goes over to the deodorant display and tells the clerk, "I need to buy some deodorant for my husband."

"Does he use the ball kind?" inquired the clerk.

"No," replied the woman. "The kind for under his arms."

One Sunday, a pastor told his congregation that the church needed some more money and asked the people to consider putting a little extra into the offering plate. He said that whoever gave the most would be able to pick out three hymns for the congregation to sing.

After the collection plates were passed around, the pastor noticed that someone had placed a new $500 bill in one. He was so excited that he immediately shared his joy with the congregation and said he'd like to personally thank the person who placed the money in the plate.

A very quiet, elderly lady all the way in the back shyly raised her hand. The pastor asked her to come to the front. Slowly she made her way to the pastor. He told her how wonderful it was that she had given so much, and said that as a reward, she should stand up and select three hymns.

Her eyes brightened as she looked over the congregation, pointed to three young men in a back pew, and said, "I'll take him and him and him."

Q: WHAT DID CINDERELLA DO ONCE SHE GOT TO THE BALL?

A: Gagged.

A businessman got on an elevator in a building. When he entered the elevator, there was a blonde already inside and she greeted him by reciting the letters, "T-G-I-F."

He smiled at her and replied, "S-H-I-T."

She looked at him, puzzled, and again said, "T-G-I-F."

He acknowledged her remark once more by answering, "S-H-I-T."

The blonde was trying to be friendly, so she smiled her biggest smile and said, as sweetly as possible, "T-G-I-F," one more time.

The man smiled back to her and once again replied, "S-H-I-T."

The blonde finally decided to explain things, and this time she said, "T-G-I-F—Thank Goodness It's Friday. Get it?"

The man answered, "S-H-I-T—Sorry, Honey, It's Thursday."

Q: WHAT'S IN *PLAYBOY*'S NEW MAGAZINE FOR MARRIED MEN?

**A:** It has the same centerfold month after month after month after month after month . . . and no celebrity interviews.

***

**Q:** WHAT'S THE DIFFERENCE BETWEEN PINK AND PURPLE?
**A:** A woman's grip.

***

A Girl Scout troop marched into a clearing in the woods and found a young couple engaged in oral sex.

"Um," the troop leader stammered, "we had better turn around. This is, um, that was actually an emergency. The young lady was performing a special kind of first aid on that man."

"Wow," one of the scouts said. "I know what merit badge I'm going for next."

***

Adam was walking around the Garden of Eden feeling lonely, so God said to him, "What is the matter?" Adam said he didn't have anyone to talk to, so God said he was going to give him a companion called "woman."

God said, "This person will cook for you and wash your clothes, and agree with all that you say. She will bear your children and never wake you in the middle of the night to care for them. She will not nag you, and will acknowledge you as the master of the house, freely admitting when she is in the wrong. She will never have a headache, and will give 'love' and compassion whenever needed."

Adam asked God, "What will this woman cost?"

God said, "An arm and a leg."

Adam asked, "What can I get for just a rib?"

A new groom goes to the doctor complaining that he can't get his wife pregnant.

"I see a lot of this," the doctor says. "You need to do it doggy style."

The man seems confused, so the doctor asks, "You do know what doggy style is, don't you?"

"Oh . . . ah . . . yeah, I guess. Of course," the man answers. "I just can't imagine my wife actually doing that."

"Many women are shy about it," the doctor says. "Just give her a few drinks and I'm sure she'll be willing."

Two months later, the man is back in the doctor's office.

"It didn't work," he says. "And now my wife is an alcoholic."

"An alcoholic?" the doctor says. "From just a few drinks."

"Hell no," he answers. "It took eight cocktails just to get her into the backyard!"

Q: WHAT DO YOU DO IF YOUR DISHWASHER BREAKS
   DOWN?
A: Kick her in the ass.

A man went to the police station wishing to speak with the burglar who had broken into his house the night before. "We'll handle the questioning, sir," said the desk sergeant.

"You don't understand," insisted the man. "I just want to know how he got into the house without waking my wife. I've been trying to do that for years!"

A newlywed couple on their honeymoon get to the hotel room. Both are from churchgoing families, and this will be their first time seeing each other undressed. The bride is blushing and seems reluctant.

"What's wrong, honey?" the husband asks.

"It's just that I'm flat-chested, and I don't want you to see me. I'm built like a schoolgirl."

"Oh, honey. So what? I'm built like a baby."

The bride smiles a sheepish grin, then undresses as her new husband pulls off his clothes. When he drops his shorts, she falls backward at the sight of his huge package.

"I . . . I thought you said you were built like a baby!"

"I am," the husband said. "Eight pounds and twenty-three inches."

Then there was a man who said, "I never knew what real happiness was until I got married; and then it was too late."

**Q:** WHY ARE WOMEN LIKE LAXATIVES?

**A:** They irritate the shit out of you.

Two old ladies are sitting on the porch smoking cigarettes when it starts to rain. The first old lady takes out a condom and wraps it around her cigarette for protection. The second old lady asks what it is and where she got it.

"You can get them at any drugstore. They're called condoms."

So the next day the second old lady goes into the drugstore and says to the clerk, "Do you sell condoms?"

The store clerk looks at her oddly and asks, "How big?"

"Oh, big enough to fit a Camel," she replies.

Pete was driving home one evening when he suddenly realized that it was his daughter's birthday and he hadn't bought her a present.

He drives to the mall, runs to the toy store, and says to the shop assistant, "How much is that Barbie in the window?"

In a condescending manner, she says, "Which Barbie? We have Barbie Goes to the Gym for $19.95, Barbie Goes to the Ball for $19.95, Barbie Goes Shopping for $19.95, Barbie Goes to the Beach for $19.95, Barbie Goes Nightclubbing for $19.95, and Divorced Barbie for $567."

Pete asks, "Why is the Divorced Barbie $567 when all the others are only $19.95?"

"That's obvious," the saleslady says. "Divorced Barbie

comes with Ken's house, Ken's car, Ken's boat, Ken's furniture . . ."

A minister is preaching the story of Creation.

"Man came first . . ." he began.

A woman at the back shouted out, "Some things never change."

Q: HOW MANY FEMINISTS DOES IT TAKE TO SCREW IN A LIGHTBULB?

A: Two. One to screw it in, and the other to write about the experience.

A guy is speeding down a highway and he gets pulled over. The cop says, "You were speeding."

The guy says, "No, I wasn't, I was going slow."

The guy's wife in the passenger seat says, "Yes, he was, Officer, he was speeding the whole time."

The guy glares at his wife and says, "Shut up!"

The cop says, "I see you don't have your seat belt on. May I ask why?"

The guy says, "Well, I saw you were about to pull me over to ask for my license, so I took it off and got out my wallet."

The guy's wife says, "No, Officer. He's had the seat belt off the whole time."

The guy says to his wife, "What the hell is wrong with you?"

The cop leans over to the wife and asks, "Is he always this nasty?"

The wife says, "Only when he's drunk."

**Q:** HOW DO YOU MAKE A HORMONE?
**A:** You refuse to pay her.

A young man is set up on a blind date and takes the girl to a carnival. She is quiet, and he finds himself making all the conversation. Finally, he asks what she'd like to do.

"I want to get weighed," she says.

So they go to the guess-your-weight booth, where the carnival man guesses the wrong weight, and she wins a prize. They wander off to the rides, and he again asks her what she'd like to do. "I want to get weighed," she says.

Back they go to the scale, although the carnival man remembers them, so he guesses the woman's weight correctly. Naturally, there's no prize this time.

The young man asks: "What do you want to do now?"

"Get weighed."

Exasperated, he refuses to spend any more money at the scales and leads her to the parking lot and drives her home. Inside the front door, the girl's roommate asks her how the date went.

"Wousy," she replies.

A couple came upon a wishing well. The husband leaned over, made a wish, and threw in a penny. The wife decided to make a wish, too. But she leaned over too far, fell into the well, and drowned.

Stunned, her husband threw his hands up in the air and said, "It really works!"

Q: WHAT'S BETTER THAN HONOR?
A: In 'er.

One day, two women are sitting on the front porch talking.

"My husband just painted our bedroom," says the first woman.

"Isn't that nice," says the second.

"My husband took me to an expensive French restaurant," the first woman says.

"Oh, isn't that nice," the second replies.

"My husband bought me a brand-new mink coat," the first woman says.

"Yes, isn't that nice," says the second woman.

The first woman finally says, "So what has your husband done for you?"

"My husband took me to an anger-management class," replies the second wife. "They taught me to say 'Isn't that nice?' instead of 'Who gives a flying fuck?' "

A guy walked into a bar with a pet alligator by his side. He put the gator up on the bar and turned to the astonished patrons.

"I'll make you an offer. I'll open this alligator's mouth and place my genitals inside. Then the gator will close his mouth for one minute. Then he'll open his mouth, and I'll remove my unit unscathed. But each of you has to buy me a drink, in return."

Everyone agreed. The man stood up on the bar, dropped his trousers, and placed his privates in the alligator's open mouth. The gator closed his mouth as the crowd gasped. After a minute, the man grabbed a beer bottle and rapped the alligator hard on the top its head. The alligator opened his mouth and the man removed his genitals, unharmed as promised. The crowd cheered and the first of his free drinks was delivered. The man stood up again and made another offer.

"I'll pay anyone $100 who's willing to give it a try." The crowd got very quiet, although after a while, a hand went up in the back of the bar.

"I'll try," said a woman, "but only if you don't hit me on the head with the beer bottle."

In the middle of a huge fight, a woman yelled at her husband, "You're gonna be really sorry! I'm going to leave you!"

"Make up your mind." he responded. "Which one is it gonna be?"

A woman was walking down the street with one of her breasts flopping out of her shirt.

"Miss," a gentleman says, "you might want to cover yourself."

She looks down then says, "Oh, shit. I left the baby on the bus!"

**Q:** WHY DO WOMEN HAVE TWO SETS OF LIPS?
**A:** So they can bitch and moan at the same time.

**Q:** HOW IS A WIFE LIKE AN ANGEL?
**A:** She's always up in the air harping on things.

A policeman pulls over a guy in a car who has been weaving from one side of the road to the other.

"Are you drunk?" the cop asks.

"Why?" the guys asks, looking into his backseat. "Is there a fat broad in here?"

A chicken and an egg lay in bed together. The chicken was smiling and smoking a cigarette, but the egg looked very distraught.

"Well," said the egg, "I guess that answers *that* question!"

**Q:** WHAT DID THE MAN SAY WHEN HIS WIFE COMPLAINED THAT HE NEVER LISTENED TO HER?

**A:** Nothing. He had no idea what she was bitching about.

A man comes home and finds his wife weeding the garden in the backyard. He pounces on her, covers her eyes, and does her from behind. After climax, she collapses face-down in the flower bed, and he becomes furious at her.

"Why are you angry?" she asks.

"Because you didn't turn around to see who it was!"

**Q:** WHY DOES EVERY MAN NEED A WIFE?

**A:** Because he can't blame everything that goes wrong on the government.

**Q:** WHAT'S THE DIFFERENCE BETWEEN BEAUTIFUL AND UGLY?

**A:** Eight beers.

**Q:** WHAT'S THE MAIN DIFFERENCE BETWEEN AN ORAL AND A RECTAL THERMOMETER?

**A:** The taste.

171

**Q:** WHAT IS THE DEFINITION OF *MIXED EMOTIONS?*

**A:** Watching your mother-in-law go off a cliff in your brand-new Lincoln.

**Q:** WHAT DID THE BLIND MAN SAY ON HIS WAY IN TO THE FISH MARKET?

**A:** "Good morning, ladies."

**Q:** HOW DO YOU PISS OFF WINNIE-THE-POOH?

**A:** Eat his honey.

**Q:** WHAT DID THE MAN THINK WHEN HE GOT A GUN FOR HIS WIFE?

**A:** That it was the best trade he ever made.

**Q:** WHY DO ONLY 2 PERCENT OF WOMEN TAKE TYPING IN COLLEGE?

**A:** The rest are hunt-'n-peckers.

A woman walks into a drugstore and asks the pharmacist if he sells condoms, size extra large.

"Yes, we do," he replies. "Would you like to buy some?"

"No," she tells him. "But do you mind if I wait around here until someone does?"

The reception had ended and the newlyweds had just sneaked off to the honeymoon resort. After an elegant supper and champagne, the groom retired to the bedroom. But the bride pulled a chair up to the balcony doors and sat there, gazing at the stars.

"Aren't you coming to bed?" the groom asked.

"No," the bride announced. "My mother told me this was going to be the most beautiful night of my life, and I don't want to miss a single minute of it."

Q: HOW DOES A TEENAGE GIRL TURN ON THE LIGHT AFTER SEX?
A: She opens the car door.

Q: HOW ARE WOMEN AND ROCKS ALIKE?
A: The flat ones are best to skip.

A couple is fooling around when they hear a key in the door. The woman breaks away and yells, "It's my husband. Quick, jump out the window."

"I can't," the man says. "We're on the thirteenth floor!"

"For heaven's sake!" cries the woman. "This is no time to be superstitious."

Q: WHAT'S THE DEFINITION OF MARRIAGE?
A: The most expensive way to have your laundry washed.

"Mr. Holt, I have reviewed this case very carefully," the divorce-court judge said. "And I have decided to give your wife $800 a week."

"That's very fair, Your Honor," the husband said. "And every now and then, I'll try to send her and the kids a few bucks myself."

A woman tells her husband that she wants to get implants to increase her breast size from a B cup to a C.

Her husband says, "You don't need a plastic surgeon to do that. I know how to do it *without* surgery."

"How?" she asks.

"Just rub toilet paper between them," he replies.

Startled, she says, "Does that make them bigger?"

"I don't know," he says. "But it worked on your ass."

A guy arrived at an old friend's house for dinner. He found that his buddy called his wife every cutesy name in the book: honey, darling, sweetheart, pumpkin, baby.

When she was in the kitchen, he leaned over to his friend and said, "I think it's nice you still call your wife all those pet names."

"To tell you the truth," his friend said, "I forgot her name about three years ago."

Q: WHY DID GOD CREATE WOMEN?
A: Because sheep can't carry beer from the fridge.

Q: WHY DID GOD CREATE BRUNETTES?
A: Neither can blondes.

At the end of an early-morning fight, and before he walks out the door, a doctor yells at his wife: "And, by the way, you're lousy in bed." He comes home that night to find her having sex with the gardener.

"What the hell are you doing?" the doctor says, stunned.

"Getting a second opinion," she replies.

A man and a widow go to City Hall to get a marriage license. While they are there, the clerk asks the woman if her previous marriage ended in death or divorce.

"I didn't know I had a choice," she replies.

A woman walks into an exotic pet store and asks about unusual pets. The young man working the counter reaches into a tank and pulls out a small frog.

"This is a special frog," he explains. "If you disrobe in front of it, it will perform oral sex."

The woman returns three days later, looking angry. "This frog doesn't do anything!"

The young man looks perplexed. "You must be doing something wrong."

"No, I'm not. I take off my clothes, and hold the frog near me, and he just stares."

"Well, let me see you try it."

Nervous, the woman complies and strips down. The frog just sits there, blinking.

"Now," the young man says to the frog while getting on his knees, "I'm only going to show you this one more time . . ."

A married couple are discussing why they're marriage is in a rut. They decide that like many married people, it's because they never go out and have fun anymore.

"Let's go out and have a good time tonight," the wife says finally.

"Okay," the husband replies. "But if you get home before I do, leave the hallway light on."

It's a mailman's last day on the job and the neighborhood is offering farewell gifts. He leaves his first stop with a box of cigars, the second with a tin of brownies, the third with a bottle of brandy. At the fourth house, a woman opens the door wearing only a rose and invites him in. They make love, then she hands him a single dollar bill.

"I can't believe I got such a great farewell gift, ma'am—especially from a married woman."

"Don't be silly," she says. "It was my husband's idea."

"You're kidding," he replies.

"No," she says. "When I asked him what we should get you as a gift, he said: 'Fuck him. Give him a dollar.' "

Two men are having a drink in a bar and are talking about their sex lives.

The first man says, "You know, I got married just so I could get laid four times a week."

"That's why I got divorced," replies the second man.

A guy is away on a business trip. He checks into his hotel and goes into the bathroom to clean up. He notices a machine on the wall with WIFE AWAY FROM HOME printed on it.

He goes out to dinner by himself, has a couple of drinks with dinner, and goes back to his hotel. When he walks into the bathroom in his room, he again notices the Wife-Away-from-Home machine. It's got a hole in it about waist-high, and a slot to put quarters into. He figures what the hell, takes out his dick, puts it in the hole, and plugs four quarters into the machine. The machine starts to whir and hum. At first it kinda stings, but then after a little while it feels pretty good, so he leaves his member in and waits to see what will happen. After a minute or two, though, it just shuts off.

Surprised, he takes his dick out and—lo and behold—there's a button sewn on the end of it!

A woman walks into a movie theater and sees a parental warning sign saying NO ONE UNDER 17 ADMITTED. So she runs back to the bar she just left and gets sixteen friends to go with her.

She offered her honor.
   He honored her offer.
   And all night long, he was on her and off her.

Q: WHY DID THE WOMAN TAKE A LADDER INTO THE BAR?
A: She heard the drinks were on the house.

Two prostitutes were riding around town with a sign on top of their car which said TWO HOOKERS—$50.

A policeman, seeing the sign, stopped them and told them they'd either have to remove the sign or go to jail.

Just then, another car passed with a sign saying JESUS LOVES YOU.

One of the girls asked the cop, "How come you don't stop them?"

"Well, that's a little different." The cop smiled. "Their sign pertains to religion."

So the two ladies of the night frowned as they took their sign down and drove off.

The following day found the same cop in the area when he noticed the two ladies driving around with a large sign on their car again. Figuring he had an easy arrest, he began to catch up with them when he noticed a new sign, which now read TWO ANGELS SEEKING PETER—$50.

Q: WHAT DID THE BLONDE SAY AFTER READING THE NAME TAG PINNED TO THE FRONT OF A CHESTY WAITRESS?

A: " 'Debbie' . . . that's cute. What did you name the other one?"

There are four nuns who die and go to Heaven. Before he'll let them in, Saint Peter asks all four how they lived and whether or not they've always been pure in mind and deed. The first nun says, "Well, Saint Peter, I've always tried, but I have to confess that I once saw a man's private parts."

Saint Peter says, "Don't worry. Do you see that Holy Water over there? Just wash your eyes in the Holy Water, and you can go into Heaven." So she does.

The second nun says, "Well, Saint Peter, although I always tried to be pure, I'm afraid I once touched a man's privates."

Saint Peter says, "Okay. Go wash your hands in the Holy Water, and you can go into Heaven, too." So she does.

At that point, the fourth nun pushes aside the third and says to Saint Peter, "Me next. If you think I'm going to gargle with that water after she washes her ass in it, you're crazy!"

Two girlfriends were speeding down the highway at well over ninety miles per hour. "Hey," asked the redhead at the wheel, "do you see any cops following us?"

The first one turned around for a long look. "As a matter of fact, I do."

"Damn!" cursed the second. "Are his flashers on?"

The first woman turned around again. "Yup . . . nope . . . yup . . . nope . . . yup . . ."

Queen Elizabeth and Dolly Parton die and go to Heaven on the same day. Saint Peter, who likes both of them, has to choose between them.

"I'm sorry, ladies," he says. "We're full up today, and I can only let one of you through the Pearly Gates."

Both are disappointed, but each is confident that she'll be the one to get in.

"How dreadful," says the Queen. "What can we do?"

Saint Peter says, "Each of you should show me what you do best, and I'll decide."

Dolly goes first, and all she does is open her blouse and let her fabulous breasts burst out. "These are my best feature," she says proudly.

Clearly impressed, Saint Peter turns to Queen Elizabeth and says, "Can you top that?"

Elizabeth drops her drawers and, shaking a bottle of cola, gives herself a douche with it.

Saint Peter waves her in, and shaking his head and turning to Dolly Parton, he says, "Sorry, Dolly. A royal flush beats a pair any day!"

A man is driving along a deserted road in winter with his wife, his kids, and his mother-in-law. Out of nowhere, a skunk runs in front of their car. He slams on the brakes but hits it anyway. He stops the car and gets out to look at the skunk, which is injured but still alive. His children are distraught.

"It's shivering," says one. "It must be cold!"

"We can't just leave it here," says another. "It'll die!"

Turning to his mother-in-law, the father says, "Put it between your legs to warm it up."

His wife turns to him and says, "But what about the smell?"

He says, "She'll just have to hold its nose!"

A blond woman goes to see her doctor, who tells her she'll have to have a Pap test. "Oh, damn," she says. "Will I have to study for it? I was never very good in school."

A woman who received a fishing rod for her birthday decides to go ice fishing to try out her gift. Early the next morning, she gets all her gear together and heads out to the ice. When she reaches her destination, she cuts a large hole in the ice and drops a line in. Suddenly she hears a voice that says: "There are no fish in there."

She moves to another spot on the ice and cuts another hole, but then the same voice speaks again and tells her there are no fish in there.

So she moves again, and once again the voice tells her there are no fish in there. She looks up and sees an irritated man staring down at her.

"How do you know there are no fish?" she asks.

The man coolly says, "Because this is a hockey rink. And by the way, you're going to have to pay for all those holes."

Q: HOW DO YOU CHANGE A WOMAN'S MIND?
A: Blow in her ear.

A businessman decides to hire a bookkeeper. He puts an ad in the newspaper, and three women apply for an interview. During the interviews, he asks each one the same question: If a customer were to send in a payment which is *double* what is owed, what would she do with the check?

The first one says she'd deposit it, and then write a check to the customer for the amount of the overpayment.

The second says she'd deposit the check and not say anything about it to anyone.

The third says she wouldn't do anything, but she'd go to her boss for advice.

Which one gets the job?

Answer: The one with the best tits.

A model wanted to sell her car, but couldn't find any buyers. She called her friend for advice, and her friend asked her how many miles were on the car's odometer.

"About 250,000," she said.

Her friend told her that was the problem. But she also said that her brother was a mechanic and could roll back the miles to whatever she wanted. So the model went to the mechanic and told him to put the odometer down to 40,000. Two days later, the model's friend asked her if the car had sold with the lower number of miles.

"Why would I sell the car?" the model said. "There are only 40,000 miles on it!"

Q: WHY DID THE WOMAN TAKE MORE THAN ONE PREGNANCY TEST?

A: Because she slept with more than one guy.

Q: WHY DID THE BLONDE GO HALFWAY TO NORWAY AND THEN TURN AROUND AND COME HOME?

**A:** It took her that long to discover that a fourteen-inch Viking was a television.

A guy out on the golf course takes a golf ball right in the crotch. Writhing in agony, he falls to the ground.

When he finally gets himself to the doctor, he says, "How bad is it, Doc? I'm going on my honeymoon next week and my fiancée is still a virgin in every way."

The doc says, "I'll have to put your penis in a splint to let it heal and keep it straight. It should be okay next week." So he takes four tongue depressors and forms a little four-sided bandage, and tapes it all together.

The guy mentions none of this to his girl. They get married, and on his honeymoon night in the motel room, she opens her blouse to reveal a gorgeous set of breasts. This is the first time he has seen them.

She says, "You'll be the first; no one has ever touched these."

As he pulls down his pants, his bride gasps. "You're a virgin, too!" she exclaims with joy. "Yours is still in the original package!"

The army officer shouted orders to a nearby soldier. The GI listened to the instructions, looked toward the firefight ahead of him, and then ran directly into the field of fire. He snatched a document case from a dead soldier and ran back to the foxhole through a hail of lethal small-weapons fire.

"Private," the officer said, "I'm recommending you for

a medal. You risked your life to save the locations of our secret warehouses."

"Warehouses!" the private shouted. "I thought you said 'whorehouses'!"